THE EMPEROR'S
GRACE

It would be all natural and possible that you would
be standing before a firing squad ... however, by the
august virtues and grace of His Majesty, The Emperor,
and also the benevolence of our military authorities,
you are still sound and alive.

Address by Lieutenant Yasuji Morimoto
Commandant, Osaka Number 5-D prisoner of war camp
December 1942

THE EMPEROR'S GRACE

Untold Stories of the Australians Enslaved in Japan during World War II

Mark Baker

MONASH UNIVERSITY PUBLISHING

The Emperor's Grace: Untold Stories of the Australians Enslaved in Japan during World War II

Monash University Publishing
Matheson Library Annexe
40 Exhibition Walk
Monash University
Clayton, Victoria 3800, Australia
publishing.monash.edu

Monash University Publishing brings to the world publications that advance the best traditions of humane and enlightened thought.

ISBN: 9781922464033 (paperback)
ISBN: 9781922464040 (pdf)
ISBN: 9781922464057 (epub)

Cover images:
Emperor Hirohito, Shōwa Emperor of Japan, in dress uniform in 1935. Source: wikipedia.
Australian POWs at Fukuoka Camp 26 photographed on 15 August 1945 – the day Japan surrendered. Source: Australian War Memorial, P03541.009.

Design: Les Thomas

A catalogue record for this book is available from the National Library of Australia.

CONTENTS

For Doug,
and all the men of C Force

PRELUDE: KURONBO

The guards called him *Kuronbo*. Black Boy. The word in Japanese is laden with racist contempt. In the prisoner of war camp on the outskirts of Kobe city, Willem Hendrik Louis Wilsterman was the biggest and strongest of the 600 Allied captives. And the only black man. This would be his death sentence.

His fellow POWs also had nicknames for him. Big Black Sam. Sambo. Or just Sam. But they liked his brashness and bravery. And they were disgusted by the way he was singled out for more than the usual quota of bashings and abuse by the Japanese guards, particularly the sadistic Ko Nishikawa.

Born in the Dutch South American colony of Surinam, 39-year-old Wilsterman had been working at Kediri in eastern Java and enlisted in KNIL (the Royal Netherlands East Indies Army) shortly before the Dutch declared war on Japan after Pearl Harbor. He left behind a wife and five children. Captured when the Japanese seized control of the East Indies following the fall of Singapore, he was one of thousands of Dutch, British and Australian POWs who were transported to work in the factories and mines of the Japanese mainland. From the moment in late 1942 that he arrived at the Osaka 5-D Camp in Kobe – whose inmates were sent to work in the nearby Kawasaki shipyard – Wilsterman was a marked man.

He was always defiant. He answered back to the guards. And he was strong. It was said he had been the sparring partner of a champion boxer before the war. The Japanese loathed everything about Wilsterman, but most of all his seemingly unbending spirit. They beat him often and fiercely. Once Nishikawa made him stand to attention, then began hitting him with a heavy ball-pein hammer. First to the left temple, then the right. Again and again. The pain was excruciating. Eventually Wilsterman fell to the ground where he was kicked mercilessly as other guards joined the attack. Time and again he would be dragged off to the guardhouse, locked in solitary confinement without proper clothing or food and held for as long as a week. Each time he was released he would return battered but unbroken.

But one night it was different.

Lieutenant Doug Lush of the Australian 8th Division Signals was the second most senior POW at the Kobe camp after fellow Australian officer Captain John Paterson. A champion athlete in Melbourne before the war, Lush admired Wilsterman's strength and physique – and his reckless defiance.

As the winter of 1943 set in, the prisoners had all been issued with second-hand overcoats by the Japanese. Soon it was discovered that several of the coats had been traded with civilian workers at the shipyard. The camp guards quickly focused their outraged attention on Wilsterman, who finally confessed to trading his coat and that of another Dutch prisoner. When the men returned from the shipyard that evening, the guards called out Wilsterman and ordered him to produce his overcoat. When he couldn't, a barrage of beatings began for him and all of his fellow prisoners.

It remained a searing memory for Lush, even in his 90s: "As I was standing waiting to dismiss the parade, Nishikawa walked straight up to me and started immediately to bash me. He knocked five of my teeth out and broke my jaw. I had to stand there and take this bashing which caused me to spit out blood as well as some of the broken teeth."[1]

Nishikawa then screamed at the prisoners to step forward as he took off his belt. Lush was then ordered to assemble the men in a series of rows. Nishikawa then moved through, belting each man in the line before the next row was ordered to more forward, and the next and the next. Over several hours each man was repeatedly beaten over the head with the leather belt.

If the punishment meted out that night, and the next, was harsh for Lush and the other men on parade, it was much more so for Willem Wilsterman, as the transcript of later war crimes hearings would record:

> The following night the accused [Nishikawa] again beat the men. The beating was brutal and an awful sight. Wilsterman had a swollen face, one eye was closed and he was bleeding from the mouth. Wilsterman was taken to the office of the camp where the accused beat him with a wooden club about two inches in diameter. Several days after the overcoat incident, the accused ordered Wilsterman to stand outside the guard house for about two hours holding a plank of wood (similar in size to a railway sleeper) above his head, and when he bent at the knees or relaxed in any way, he was hit on the head and face with a wooden sword by the accused.[2]

Worse was to follow. Wilsterman was placed in solitary confinement in a small cage that served as the camp jail and denied even the meagre daily food ration. Warrant Officer Des Mulcahy and the other prisoners did what they could to alleviate his suffering. They were allowed to bring him just two rice balls a day. It was mid-winter and when the guards were changed each hour during the night they would strip the prisoner naked and douse him with icy water.[3]

Wilsterman died on 15 December 1943. His death was recorded by his tormentors as "heart failure". But he had been starved, tortured and frozen to death.

When Japan seized control of most of South-East Asia in early 1942, they captured 140,000 Allied military personnel. By the end of the war, more than 30,000 of those POWs had died from disease, starvation, violent abuse and exhaustion as slave labourers in brutal work camps. Among them were 22,000 Australians, most of them trapped by the fall of Singapore. More than a third would perish.

About 36,000 of the Allied prisoners were sent to work in Japan – another 11,000 were lost during the voyage when the ships carrying them were unwittingly sunk by Allied aircraft and submarines. Those who got through included about 3800 Australians. One in 10 of the prisoners in Japan would die there. Those who survived would carry the physical and emotional scars for the rest of their lives.[4]

This is the story of many, recounted through the indelible memories of a few.

Chapter 1

BROTHERS IN ARMS

To 'Uncle John' in appreciation of your guidance,
tolerance and consideration in 1940, 1941 and 1942,
your good companionship in 1943, 1944 and 1945 and
the promise of an enduring friendship in the years to
come ... from your two 'nephews'.

*Hand-drawn greeting card to John Paterson from Doug Lush
and Ken Trumble, Kobe POW camp, 1 January 1945*[1]

The life of John Frederick Douglas Lush began amid tragedy and hardship, but adversity would help steel him for the ordeals that lay ahead. He was born on 24 May 1918, Empire Day, less than six months before the end of World War I. Lush's father had migrated from England in 1909, leasing a property at Merredin in the wheat-belt country 150 miles east of Perth. The land and climate were harsh but Jack Lush was tough and resolute. In 1912, he marred Ruby Cohen, the daughter of a large West Australian family. Together they worked hard with little money, determined to make their own luck.

A few months after the birth of the boy who would be known as Douglas, Ruby fell pregnant again. As the second birth approached, she began to haemorrhage and had to be rushed to the Merredin hospital – a 17-mile journey over rough tracks by horse and gig. The journey ended with both mother and child dead on arrival at the hospital. Unable to cope alone, Jack Lush passed on his surviving son to be cared for by the families of neighbouring farmers. Soon it became clear that this temporary arrangement could not continue and it was resolved that the little boy would move permanently to live with his childless aunt and uncle in Melbourne.

Ruby Lush's sister Agnes and her husband, George Cassels, lived in the south-eastern Melbourne suburb of Caulfield. George, a carpenter, had built their house in Nyora Grove which was then still surrounded by paddocks. The family was supplied with fresh milk each day from a dairy farm nearby. Vegetables were delivered by a Chinese market gardener and a bakery boy brought bread and buns. Another regular visitor would arrive shouting "Rabbito!", carrying a hessian sack of rabbits that he would skin on demand.

Lush showed aptitude both on and off the sporting field. At the age of 13, his academic prowess earned him a place at the prestigious Melbourne High School where he was enrolled in 1932 and 1933. He would be inspired by one of his teachers, Bill Woodfull, the Australian Test cricket captain. One day, while returning home from a cricket match, Lush was approached by the manager of the Guardian Assurance Company who asked whether he would like a job. The traineeship with Guardian – where he was chosen from a field of 100 applicants – was the start of what would be a lifetime career in the insurance industry.

By the mid-1930s, Doug Lush was emerging as a champion hurdler with his athletics team, the Melbourne Harriers. In 1938 he was selected in the Australian team for the Empire Games in Sydney in the sprints and hurdles – alongside friends John Park, Orm Watt and Ted Best whom he had met through the Power House athletics club in Albert Park and the affiliated Lord Somers Camp on the Mornington

Peninsula. Another star athlete in their circle was Jim Cairns, who was Victorian broad-jump and decathlon champion – before achieving even greater fame as a leader of the anti-Vietnam War movement in the 1960s and then Deputy Prime Minister of Australia in the Whitlam government.[2] And it was through Power House that Doug Lush would meet the man who would have the greatest influence on his life – particularly when war broke out in 1939.

Stewart Austin Embling was a distinguished athlete, coach and sports administrator who would be chosen as starter for the marathon at the 1956 Melbourne Olympic Games. Embling was not only a passionate sportsman but also an officer in the militia – and he would inspire Lush, 11 years his junior, in both directions. Like many young men of his generation, Lush's response to the declaration of war in Europe was instinctive and immediate: "It was automatic. All my mates enlisted and so did I. In these days it was king and country. It was a foregone conclusion that we would fight for the country and we all joined up."[3]

When Lush enlisted in the army in June 1940, he chose the Signals Corps, inspired by Stewart Embling who had enlisted with Signals a month earlier. But their military careers would soon take sharply different directions. Major Embling offered the newly commissioned Lieutenant Lush a position at the School of Signals in Palestine. But this would have required Lush to resign his commission and travel to the Middle East as a warrant officer, so he declined. The two men would not see each other again for another five years. Rising to the rank of lieutenant colonel, Embling would serve through some of the biggest battles of the North Africa campaign, being twice mentioned in dispatches. He was later attached to the Signals headquarters staff in Melbourne before being posted to New Guinea. After the war, Embling would end his distinguished military career as Colonel Commandant of the Signals Corps. And Doug Lush would name his only son after his friend and mentor.

As he prepared to go to war, Lush had one more important task to complete. Dorothy Daisy Richmond was a pretty and vivacious young woman whom Lush had met at the dances at The Palais in St Kilda. He was soon in love with the woman who would go on to become a model and radio actress. Before he left for army training in New South Wales, they were married.

John Paterson had spent almost half his life in part-time military service when the war began. Born the youngest of four children in the Melbourne suburb of Kensington, he had joined the militia at the age of 19, in 1923, serving with the Australian Engineers' Signal Service. He received an immediate commission as lieutenant and was promoted to captain four years later before being appointed acting adjutant and quartermaster of the 3rd Division Signals.

After training as an accountant, Paterson joined the Vacuum Oil Company, the first American oil company to establish operations in Australia. He took part in the company's rapid expansion in the 1930s after it merged with Standard Oil and began the journey that would, 30 years later, give birth to Mobil, a brand first patented by Vacuum in 1899.

In 1929, Paterson married Ethel Sylvia Blumer, who worked in the administration of the Victorian Government's Department of Agriculture. They settled in the Melbourne suburb of Balwyn and their first and only child, Janet, was born in 1931.

With the outbreak of war imminent, John Paterson, like the many others with extensive service in the militia, was called back from the military reserves. Three weeks before Britain – and Australia – declared war on Germany, he was back on duty with the 3rd Division Signals. On 7 July 1941, he was attached with the newly formed 8th Division Signals. A natural leader who was popular and respected by the men under his command, his strengths would help save the lives of many of them in the harrowing years that lay ahead.

Hugh Trumble is remembered as one of the greatest bowlers in the history of Australian cricket. An off-spinner who could also hold his own with the bat, Trumble captained Australia to victory in two Test series and twice scored hat-tricks at Test level. When he retired from cricket in the early 1900s, he had a total of 141 Test wickets to his name – a world record that stood for many years.

In 1902, by then a 31-year-old national hero, he met and married a 19-year-old Queenslander, Florence Christian. They would have eight children – six boys and two girls – many of whom would be given their mother's maiden name as their middle name. In April 1919, when Hugh was manager of a bank branch in High Street, Kew, twin boys were born: Robert William, who would became a noted musician and composer, and Kenneth Christian.

Ken Trumble was a fine athlete like his father, excelling at cricket, baseball and golf. Much of his childhood was spent ranging around the grandstands and hallowed turf of the MCG after his father became manager of the Melbourne Cricket Club. On finishing school at Trinity Grammar, Ken got a job as a junior clerk with Imperial Chemical Industries. Between the wars, ICI had emerged as Britain's biggest chemicals conglomerate and played a leading role in the development of revolutionary plastics including Perspex, polyethylene and terylene. As soon as he turned 18, he also joined the militia, with the 3rd Division

Signals. In June 1940, by then a sergeant, he enlisted for war service, his papers signed by Captain Stewart Embling.

Doug Lush, John Paterson and Ken Trumble had first met in 1938 while serving in the militia in Melbourne. In war and captivity their destinies would be bonded and they would become lifelong friends.

Chapter 2

TO WAR

Land of sickness, sin and sorrow
An inch of rain, perhaps two tomorrow
Singapore ear, footrot rife
Sooner be home with my darling wife
Chinese heaven, Aussie hell
Bastard country fare thee well.

Anonymous Australian soldier's lament, 1942

In July 1940 a small group of men drawn from several states across Australia arrived at the Casula army camp, 22 miles south-west of Sydney, to form the nucleus of the 8th Division Signals. The selected officers and NCOs were put under the command of Lieutenant Colonel J.H. Thyer. Jim Thyer was as raw to senior command as most of the men in his charge were to military life, but he soon was to prove an exemplary leader.

Born the son of a policeman in the small town of Natimuk in Victoria's Wimmera region, Thyer had entered the Royal Military College, Duntroon, in February 1915, just weeks before the Anzac landings at Gallipoli. After graduating in 1917 and being commissioned as a lieutenant, he was sent to England for further training but the war was to end before he saw action. After returning to Australia, Thyer served in a series of staff and regimental postings, slowly rising to the rank of major in 1936. Seconded to the Australian Imperial Force (AIF) in April 1940 he was promoted to lieutenant colonel three months later, just before his arrival at Casula. He had hand-picked the men in his charge after touring the country during the preceding weeks. Among the handful of Victorians he had chosen to join the 39 foundation members of the unit was Lieutenant J.F.D. Lush, who was given charge of No. 1 Company, 'C' Section.

Conditions at Casula were spartan and the basic training was tough. The mid-winter weather was intensely cold but the men had to bathe in open-air ablution blocks with no hot water. Reveille was at 7am followed by breakfast at 8am. Everyone then fell in for an hour of parades and drill instruction under the stern eye of the Regimental Sergeant Major, Warrant Officer Noel May. After two hours of lectures on administration, tactics and technical matters, lunch was served at noon. The afternoons were occupied with physical training and organised games, during which Doug Lush's athletic prowess was on display. The evening meal was followed by two more hours of lectures or exercises in night manoeuvres. Then it was lights out at 10pm.

It was a strenuous life that tested the men physically, intellectually and spiritually. "We assessed one another in those days and the knowledge we gained we remembered later and solved many problems by it," the regimental history would later recount. "We all learned to respect our fellows; we learned the virtues as well as the discomforts of discipline; we became united so that we could better withstand hard knocks which came our way."[1]

While the training proceeded at Casula, drafts of recruits were being selected and given initial training at depots throughout Australia, but predominantly in New South Wales. On 27 July the unit was relocated to the bigger army base at nearby Liverpool and the new recruits began to arrive from around the country. At the first full parade, Colonel Thyer laid out the program that would unfold over the following weeks: elementary drill, small arms training, anti-gas training, military administration and law and 'hardening' exercises: "In a nutshell, it was to be 'six weeks on the square'." From there on, the rank and file were paraded directly under Lieutenant Lush and the other section officers two or three times a day.

A group of about 90 prospective non-commissioned officers (NCOs) was selected for a special course of instruction under the direction of Thyer's second-in-command, Major Jim McKinlay. The Perth-born officer of Scottish ancestry had risen from private to lieutenant with the 4th Division Signals in World War I, was wounded at Gallipoli and won the Military Medal for gallantry on the Western Front in 1917. If life was tough during those weeks for the regular recruits, it was something else for the prospective NCOs. In the second week at Liverpool, the 'slave market' was convened, as the three company commanders haggled over the allocation of more than 80 men to their respective units.

After several months of intensive and mostly monotonous preparation, the signals companies were sent, in November, to Bathurst and the so-called 'fattening paddocks'. The newly-built training camp, on the outskirts of the provincial city, was a welcome change of scenery and there the training became more technical than physical, to the relief of all. In the down times, there were sports to be played, sight-seeing visits, dances in town and Sunday evening entertainments provided by local volunteers – after church services had been attended. There were additional attractions for those with seniority: "The officers of the unit entertained in a modest way and endeavoured to brighten the lives of some of the hard-working nurses from the camp hospital. Some individuals were admitted to hospital as patients, with the alleged aim of furthering this praiseworthy cause!"[2] Each month the men were granted four days leave, sufficient for most of those from the eastern states to make a quick trip home.

Towards Christmas, the men received a visit from the man who would lead them to war, Major General Gordon Bennett, the General Officer Commanding the 8th Division. Bennett was impressed by what he saw. Then, after eight days home leave for Christmas, and a memorable New Year's Eve concert in which many of the men revealed rare talents for song, dance and comedy – well-lubricated with free-flowing beer from the quartermaster's store – the first word came that their deployment was imminent. After a three-day bivouac to test their field training, the men were granted what would be their final leave. On their return, a short period of hectic activity ensued: "Rolls were prepared, revised, corrected and at length typed in quintuplicate. Indenture discs were marked, checked, strung and at length issued. Service dress was withdrawn from all personnel warned for embark-ation. Tropical kit was issued in its stead."[3]

On 29 January 1941 a ceremonial parade was ordered. It would be the last time that the men would fall in as an entire establishment. Colonel Thyer took the salute and addressed the unit "in a manner befitting the occasion" – announcing that a large part of the group would shortly embark for service overseas and that the remainder would then become attached, each section to its appropriate formation, until such time as all were in turn embarked for active service. "The solemnity of this ceremony was not lost upon those present," wrote the regimental historians.

After final medical examinations and kit inspections – and the ominous task of making wills – the men spent their last night in camp on Saturday 1 February. At daylight the next morning, the first flight was already on its way to Sydney and the waiting naval convoy that would transport them to war.

The Australian Government had resolved to send the 8th Division to Malaya. Major General Bennett and his senior headquarters staff, including Colonel Thyer, flew ahead of their men to Singapore. They were followed by about 6000 troops from the 22nd Infantry Brigade who sailed from Sydney aboard the *Queen Mary*. The brigade comprised the 2/18th, 2/19th and 2/20th Infantry Battalions and the 2/10th Field Artillery Regiment and supporting units including Doug Lush and his fellow signallers and 43 nurses with the 2/10th Australian General Hospital and the 2/4th Casualty Clearing Station. The men of the 22nd would be joined by the 27th Infantry Brigade in August 1941. The 8th Division's third brigade – the 23rd – remained in Australia and its forces were deployed through the islands of Timor, Ambon and New Britain when Singapore fell to the Japanese.

The 22nd Brigade was commanded by Brigadier Harold Burfield Taylor, who had served with the First AIF in World War I and twice won the Military Cross for bravery. Between the wars, Taylor led a series of militia units culminating in his command of the 5th Militia Brigade. An analytical chemist in civilian life, he was awarded a Doctorate of Science in 1925 and in 1934 became Deputy Government Analyst for New South Wales.

The *Queen Mary* was a grand way to go to war. The 81,000-ton pride of the Cunard fleet was the most luxurious liner of her day. She held the record for the fastest crossing of the Atlantic before being requestioned for war service in 1939 and painted battleship grey. The first Australian contingent to be deployed in South-East Asia began boarding on 2 February 1941 as the grand liner rode at anchor off

Bradley's Head, site of Taronga Park Zoo. The contingent was given the code name 'Elbow Force' but attempts to keep their destination secret were compromised somewhat when the milling crowd on the waterfront saw crates piled high for loading marked "Elbow Force, Singapore".

Shortly before they embarked, the Governor-General, Lord Gowrie, came aboard to say farewell and meet all the officers. Major Reginald Bridgland, the Officer Commanding Signals, presented each of the captains and then each of the lieutenants, including Doug Lush and Ken Trumble, in turn. Finally, on 4 February, the *Queen Mary* weighed anchor and turned towards Sydney Heads accompanied by the 45,000-ton *Aquitania* and the 36,000-ton Dutch liner *Nieuw Amsterdam* carrying troops to the Middle East.

The convoy carried a total of 12,000 members of the AIF. "Their cheers mingled with those of many thousands of spectators ashore and afloat, the toots of ferries and tugboats, the screams of sirens, and the big bass of *Queen Mary*'s foghorn as the convoy steamed down the harbour and through the Heads," official historian Lionel Wigmore would write. "Despite the brave showing of the farewell, it impressed on many more deeply than before the extent to which Australia was committed to a war on the other side of the world while it showed signs of spreading to the Pacific, and possible to her own soil."[4]

After clearing the Heads, the liners turned south with their escort, the light cruiser HMAS *Hobart*. The *Queen Mary* quickly picked up speed to her 30-knot maximum to dodge any lurking enemy submarines. Two days into their voyage, the convoy was joined by the *Mauretania* out of Melbourne. The course charted to Singapore was a huge diversion. The convoy sailed due south to a point well below Tasmania before crossing south of the Great Australian Bight to join another group of ships that had gathered off Fremantle for the final stage of the passage to Malaya.

While the *Queen Mary* was now officially a troop transport, the amenities were still luxurious, especially for officers such as Lieutenants Lush and Trumble. There were cabins with private bathrooms, a cinema, swimming pools and other recreational areas out of bounds to other ranks. A choice of wet canteens offered drinks at very cheap prices. There were nightly cabarets in the ship's ballroom where the nurses were welcome, if accompanied by an officer. Matrons Olive Paschke and Irene Drummond gave the nurses in their charge great latitude, asking only that they return to their quarters "at a reasonable hour". From 8 February, a shipboard newspaper called the *X-Press* was published daily. Olive Paschke called her nurses together and told them she would "rather not read about them in its pages".[5]

Since the departure from Sydney and well into their voyage, the final destination had, at least officially, remained a secret except among the most senior officers. There was little doubt that they were not headed for the Middle East when, in January, the men's service dress had been replaced with tropical kit. The charade abruptly ended when a case of books burst open while the convoy was docked at Fremantle, revealing hundreds of copies of a slim volume entitled *Notes on Malaya*. Jack Lush would travel down from the farm at Merredin to say goodbye to his son, but arrived a couple of hours too late.

After the convoy departed Fremantle, in convoy with several Australian warships and Dutch transport vessels, they steamed at a slower, uniform speed to match the capacity of smaller vessels in the flotilla. Around mid-morning on Valentine's Day, as they passed the Cocos Islands, the *Queen Mary* suddenly gathered speed and, with her foghorn blasting intermittently, circled the convoy before turning to the north-west, escorted by the British destroyer HMS *Durban*, on course for Singapore.

Signaller Lloyd Ellerman, from Young, New South Wales, was captivated by the spectacle: "In a very dramatic and impressive move, the *'Mary'* broke away from the escort and other vessels and almost doubled its speed to make a dash for Singapore. The huge ship throbbed with the increased power as it thrust itself through the Indian Ocean waters. We were thrilled to be a part of the excitement and we felt confident that no submarine or surface raider would have any hope of running us down."[6]

Three days later, on 18 February 1941, the *Queen Mary* docked at the big British naval base on the northern coast of Singapore island facing the Johore Causeway. It was the first time an Australian force had set foot in the Straits Settlements and the moment was marked with suitable fanfare, as the Signals Corps history recorded: "The Manchester Regiment was stationed on the wharf and their band played. At the end of the first musical selections, there was tumultuous applause from the troop decks. The bandsmen were gratified by the acknowledgment, but unprepared for the shower of Australian pennies that followed."[7]

Before daylight the next morning, almost the entire force was aboard trains headed for various destinations "up country" on the Malayan peninsula. Lieutenant Lush and J Section accompanied the 22nd Brigade headquarters staff to Port Dickson, a large township 30 miles south of Kuala Lumpur famed for its beauty and sweeping beaches. They were quartered in the Malay Regiment lines, in a rural setting on the outskirts of the town. Lush established a Signals office as soon as 'Jug' section arrived in Port Dickson and the unit was recognised as probably the first to be engaged in active Signal duties in Malaya.

For all members of 'Elbow' Force Signals, the arrival in Malaya ushered in a period of intense activity in a strange new land. The humid climate, the strange fauna, the lush vegetation and the mixed Malay, Indian and Chinese population with their different languages and customs were all a great novelty to most of the men. But while the location was intriguing and the natives were friendly, some of the new food was not always to the Australians' taste, as Roger Maynard would record in his book, *Hell's Heroes*:

> The locals used to describe the most common dish served up as 'yak' – not the beast of burden but an unpalatable mixture of rice and prunes. Thanks to a letter home that somehow evaded the 2/20th's official censor, a concerned mother even took up her son's case with her local MP. As recounted by Don Wall in 'Singapore and Beyond', when news of the parliament's involvement eventually got back to Malaya, an officer walked into B Company's mess hall and demanded to know if anybody had a complaint. Private Jack Kitchener, an Aborigine from Naremburn in Sydney, stunned all present by standing up and replying, 'Yes sir – this tucker's not fit for a blackfella!'[8]

Friendships grew quickly with the Malay troops. Soon the Australians were being invited to local homes and to attend weddings and other celebrations. The bonds grew as the men trained together, venturing into the jungles and waterways of the hinterland on exercises. On one exercise created by Doug Lush to keep the men fit and active, they travelled down the Keneboi and Triang rivers on bamboo rafts – a voyage that took from dawn on one day until 11 the next morning for the stragglers. Some of the rafts were smashed in the torrents and gear lost but such experiences were invaluable in giving the Australians familiarity with the terrain in which they would soon have to fight.

Sports provided a popular diversion from the growing workload of the signallers. Athletes from J section, led by Lieutenant Lush, formed a team in the 22nd Brigade sports competition that "covered itself in glory".[9] At a combined sports event in Kuala Lumpur in June, Lush would take honours in the 220-yard sprint and his section would win the relay and take aggregate points for the meeting.

Among other friendships forged in those first months at Port Dickson were those with the nurses of the 2/4 Casualty Clearing Station who also were stationed there. The small nursing team was led by Matron Irene Drummond, who had worked at the Broken Hill Hospital before enlisting in October 1940. Drummond and her colleagues were soon to become some of the most infamous victims of the Japanese invasion of South-East Asia. Of the nine young women in the team, only one – South Australian Mavis Hannah – would survive the war.

Soon after the nurses fled the fall of Singapore in February 1942, the small freighter *Vyner Brooke* on which they were travelling was bombed and sunk by Japanese aircraft in the straits off Sumatra. Two of the 2/4 nurses – Kathleen 'Kit' Kinsella and Jess Dorsch – drowned. The rest struggled ashore and were soon taken prisoner by the Japanese. Four, including Drummond, had the tragic misfortune to be among 22 Australian nurses who washed up on a beach at Banka Island where they were soon rounded up by a company of Japanese troops. As the women were lined up and ordered to walk back into the shallows, Drummond called out: "Chin up, girls! I'm proud of you all and I love you all."[10] Moments later she was killed by a barrage of machine-gun fire along with 2/4 nurses Peggy Wilmot, Elaine Balfour-Ogilvy and Peggy Farmaner.

Irene Drummond's final, brave words would be preserved for history by Vivian Bullwinkel, the only Australian to survive the Radji Beach massacre. Seriously wounded but still alive, Bullwinkel lay still in the water, feigning death until the attackers left the beach. After hiding in the nearby jungle for several days, Bullwinkel was taken prisoner by other Japanese soldiers, surviving more than three years in captivity to return home to Australia and bear witness to the shocking fate of her fellow nurses. Two more of Irene Drummond's team were not so fortunate. Both Dora Gardam and Mina Raymont died in the squalid POW camps of Sumatra.

In late July, Colonel Thyer was promoted to General Bennett's headquarters staff and replaced as commander of the Signals unit by Lieutenant Colonel Charles Kappe. Born in Ballarat, where he had commanded the Ballarat High School cadet corps, Kappe had entered the Royal Military College, Duntroon, towards the end of World War I in 1918. Between the wars, he had served in a range of engineering and Signals postings and attended the legendary British staff college at Quetta (under the then colonel and later field marshal Bernard Montgomery) before commanding the Royal Australian Engineers in Queensland. Kappe would distinguish himself by writing a 200,000-word history of the Malayan campaign as a prisoner of war in Changi and in Thailand between 1942 and 1945.

Within days of the leadership change at Port Dickson, Kappe received a telephone call advising him that an aircraft was standing by to take him to Singapore. The decision had been made to relocate the headquarters and all of the division's units to Johore. Doug Lush's J Section was ordered to move from Port Dickson to Mersing, on the remote south-east coast of the peninsula. The British and Australian commanders believed the coastline near Mersing was the most likely target for an enemy amphibious landing and therefore crucial to the ultimate defence of Johore and Singapore, as the Signals history would recount:

Once established in the Mersing-Jemaluang area, the Japanese could drive west across the peninsula or advance south-west direct on Johore Bahru, or combine both movements. An advance westwards would have paid handsomely in the capture of the airfields at Kahang, Klang and Batu Pahat, the important road and rail centre at Kluang and the road junction at Ayer Hitam; whilst an advance down the east coast road through Mawai could quickly threaten Singapore.[11]

Only three roads ran from Johore Bahru, the state capital sited just across the narrow strait from Singapore island, where Bennett's headquarters was now established. One road ran to the west coast, another to the north, and the third, which was not sealed, to the east coast at Mersing. Except for a few rubber plantations near the main roads, the state was mostly jungle. Civil telephone and telegraph communications were negligible except for the main trunk route which followed the railway to the north. When the Signals units first arrived in August, only two pairs of telephone wires connected Mersing with Johore Bahru. The men were now faced with a heavy workload to quickly upgrade communications. Soon J Section would be responsible for maintaining more than 100 miles of cabling, much of it traversing areas of dense jungle that was still the habitat of wild elephants and tigers. While the signallers toiled, the infantry battalions began reinforcing defences. Hundreds of men were drafted in to fell timber, shovel sand, build stockades and erect hundreds of yards of barbed-wire fencing around the small town. As the Mersing River stood in the way of any advance by land from the north, anti-tank and anti-personnel minefields were laid along its estuary and the north–south road.[12]

While the 22nd Brigade group worked to strengthen defensive positions around Mersing, a detachment was sent to Endau, a smaller township 20 miles to the north on the border between Johore and

Pahang states, to counter any possible move by the invaders to bypass the coastal defenders by moving up the Endau River. By the end of November, all of the preparations were complete and all of the new communications were ready and had been tested in day and night exercises. After three months of exhausting toil, the men of J Section, working alongside the men of Lieutenant Reg Hastings' E Section, had completed construction of Signal Office dugouts and the line system in the 22nd Brigade group area at Mersing.

On 1 December the code word 'Seaview' was issued to all Australian forces, signifying the order "Adopt Second Degree of Readiness". All leave ceased, vulnerable point guards were strengthened, coast and anti-aircraft defences were manned, local volunteers were called up and all headquarters began operating around the clock. After five tense and impatient days, the long-awaited code word 'Raffles' was received at 3.15pm on 6 December. War was at hand.

The Signals team was assembled at 4pm and addressed by the CO. He told the men that by their high standard of discipline and efficiency they had already earned a reputation second to none and that he personally had no doubt that they would all acquit themselves well whatever their ultimate fate.[13] At 6pm the Advanced Signal Group moved out of the base camp with its office, wireless and line detachments. Twenty minutes later, the administrative group under Major Colin Johnstone and parties to reinforce the Signal centres at Klang and Kota Tinggi were on their way. As the other sections dispersed across the hinterland, J Section moved to its battle headquarters at the 81.5 mile peg on the Mersing Road.

The next day the dramatic news came that the invasion of Malaya and the bombing of Singapore had begun.

Chapter 3

THE FALL

It was these men who delayed the Japanese drive
southwards. It was they who won for Australia
the precious weeks and months that enabled her,
with the aid of the United States, to transform this
country into a mighty base from which, at length,
were launched those operations which ended
in the occupation of Japan.

Rohan Rivett, Behind Bamboo[1]

At 8.45am on 7 December 1941 a Catalina flying boat from 205
Squadron RAF commanded by Flying Officer Edwin Beddell intercepted a Japanese naval force moving across the Gulf of Siam, about
150 miles north-east of the Malayan state of Kelantan. Beddell, a
31-year-old serving with the RAF Volunteer Reserve, and his seven-
member crew, had been scrambled to verify earlier sporadic sightings of
Japanese warships. Before the Catalina was able to radio its coordinates
back to base, they were attacked by Japanese Aichi E13A Jake reconnaissance float planes catapulted from the tender *Kamikawa Maru*.

As the Catalina sought desperately to evade fire, the attack was
joined by five Ki-27 fighters. After several hits, a long burst of fire from
one of the fighters piloted by Ensign Eiichi Ogata saw the Catalina
explode into a ball of fire and plunge 400 feet into the sea. All of the

crew was reported killed by the Japanese, thereby becoming the first Allied combat casualties of the war in Asia. Among them was Sergeant Colin 'Ike' Treloar, a 21-year-old navigator from Adelaide, who had enlisted in the RAAF a year earlier.

Despite other compelling evidence that the Japanese were preparing to invade, the British prevaricated. Air Marshal Sir Robert Brooke-Popham, commanding officer of the British forces in the Far East, feared that the Japanese armada was trying to provoke a British attack and thereby provide a pretext for them to go to war. As 7 December unfolded – and the first Allied casualties aboard Beddell's Catalina remained unconfirmed – Brooke-Popham held back from launching Operation Matador, the British plan to destroy an invasion force before it landed. He decided to delay the operation, at least overnight. It would prove to be a catastrophic miscalculation.

Soon after midnight, Indian soldiers patrolling the beaches near Kota Bharu, the capital of Kelantan, saw three large shadows looming across the water. The transport ships *Awazisan Maru*, *Ayatosan Maru*, and *Sakura Maru* dropped anchor less than two miles off the coast. They were carrying 5500 troops of the Takumi Detachment – most of them veterans of the war in China – led by Major General Hiroshi Takumi. Simultaneously, larger landings were under way at Singora and Pattani in southern Thailand. As the troops began surging ashore aboard small landing craft, defying rough seas and strong winds, waves of Japanese aircraft were on their final approach to Pearl Harbor in Hawaii. The Pacific war had begun.

The Japanese commander of the attack on Malaya was the bull-headed, tough-talking Lieutenant General Tomoyuki Yamashita. One of the most brilliant generals of his generation, Yamashita had led a division fighting insurgents in northern China in the late 1930s.

He had argued in vain that Japan should end the conflict with China and maintain peaceful relations with the United States and Britain. In December 1940, Yamashita was sent on a six-month secret military mission to Germany and Italy to study their warfare tactics. During the mission, he had meetings with both Adolf Hitler and Benito Mussolini. For the operations against Malaya, his 25th Japanese Army had more than 125,000 men. He also had the support of a naval air group with 459 aircraft and the Japanese Navy's Southern Command, comprised of a battle cruiser, 10 destroyers and five submarines.

From the outset, the British forces in northern Malaya were out-numbered and outmanoeuvred. In Kelantan, the defending force was the 8th Indian Infantry Brigade supported by four 3.7 inch howitzers of the 21st Mountain Battery. The 3/17th Battalion, Dogra Regiment, had responsibility for the 10-mile stretch of coast where the Japanese landed. The British had fortified the sector with land mines, barbed wire and pillboxes. As the first Japanese troops came ashore, the Dogras opened intense fire with artillery and machine guns. Yamashita's senior strategist, Colonel Masanobu Tsuji, described what happened next:

> As daylight came, it became impossible to move under the heavy enemy fire at point blank range. Officers and men instinctively dug with their hands into the sand and hid their heads in the hollows. Then they burrowed until their shoulders, and event-ually their whole bodies, were under cover. Their positions were so close to the enemy that they could throw hand grenades into the loopholes in the pillboxes. All the time they were using their steel helmets to dig their way further forward, with their swords dragging on the sand beside them. Eventually they reached the wire entanglements. Those with wire-cutters got to work, but they had scarcely commenced when there was a thunderous report and clouds of dust threw up completely obscuring the view for a time. The attackers had reached the British mined zone. Moving

over corpses the wire cutters kept at their work. Behind them followed a few men, piling up the sand ahead of them with their steel helmets and creeping forward like moles. The enemy soldiers manning the pillboxes fought desperately. Suddenly one of our men covered a loophole with his body and a group of the moles sprung to their feet in a spurt of sand and rushed into the enemy's fortified position. Hand grenades flew and bayonets flashed, and amid the sound of warcries and calls of distress, in a cloud of black smoke the enemy's front line was captured.[2]

After hours of vicious hand-to-hand fighting, the Japanese began to gain the upper hand and the Dogras were forced to retreat further to their defences in front of the Kota Bharu airfield. Reserve troops were brought forward to reinforce the Dogras. At 10.30am the brigade commander, Brigadier Billy Key, ordered an attempt to retake the lost beaches with the 2/12th Frontier Force Regiment attacking from the south and the 1/13th Frontier Force Rifles attacking from the north. The fighting on the beaches was heavy with both sides suffering substantial casualties. The British forces made some progress but were unable to close the breach. In the afternoon, a second attack went in but failed again to turn the tide.

Meanwhile, 1 Squadron RAAF based at Kota Bharu airfield had sent 10 Lockheed Hudson bombers to attack the Japanese transports still positioned off the coast. In 17 sorties flown, two Hudsons were shot down and three badly damaged. One, flown by 22-year-old Flight Lieutenant John Graham Leighton-Jones, crashed into a fully laden landing craft after being hit while strafing the beachhead, killing 60 Japanese soldiers on board. Only five Hudson bombers remained airworthy at the end of the battle. By dusk on 8 December, the airfield had been evacuated and Japanese troops were now able to infiltrate between the British units. The Japanese would later concede that the landings at Kota Bharu involved some of the most violent fighting of the whole Malayan campaign – with an estimated 300 of their men killed and another 500 wounded. But the Takumi Detachment was now firmly ashore in Malaya and ready to begin its advance south to Singapore.

Within 10 days of the Japanese landings, all of the northern airfields were in enemy hands, many of the RAAF bombers had been lost and the fighter aircraft had been shown to be woefully inferior to the Japanese Zeros. And the ground fighting was inflicting heavy casualties. On 10 December the battleship *Prince of Wales* and the cruiser *Repulse* – the two great warships whose arrival from Europe in early December had "caused a wave of relief and even elation to sweep over Malaya"[3] – had been sunk off Kuantan as they headed north to engage the Japanese fleet. Admiral Sir Tom Phillips and Captain John Leach refused to abandon the flagship and were lost along with 845 other men. It was one of the greatest disasters in the history of the Royal Navy. As historian Mark Clisby would write: "Within a short time the Japanese had an unchallenged mastery of the sea and air."[4] Soon that mastery would extend to the Malayan mainland.

By mid-January 1942, the main British force – III Indian Corps – had been pushed back to the edge of Johore and morale was crumbling. The Australian 22nd Brigade and supporting units remained deployed on the east coast around Mersing while the 27th Brigade was positioned towards the west coast of the peninsula. The Australian infantry would have their baptism of fire in a carefully planned ambush of advancing Japanese forces near the township of Gemas, about 150 miles north-west of Singapore. It would be one of the few successes for Allied forces in the Pacific in 1942.

Following the disastrous Battle of Slim River, just north of Kuala Lumpur, on 6–8 January – during which two Indian brigades were virtually annihilated – the British commander in Malaya, Lieutenant General Arthur Percival, resolved that the best his army could do, pending the arrival of expected reinforcements, was to attempt to slow the Japanese advance and hold Johore. The brunt of this strategy now fell to the Australians and, in particular, the 2/30th Battalion commanded by the audacious Lieutenant Colonel Frederick 'Black Jack' Galleghan. The battalion had been formed in November 1940 in Tamworth, its men drawn predominantly from New South Wales. Well-trained, and soon to prove their mettle, they would become known as Galleghan's Greyhounds.

General Bennett, now leading a multinational force codenamed Westforce, planned to spearhead the counterattack by staging an ambush near the Gemencheh River, seven miles west of Gemas. The position consisted of a main road leading to a wooden bridge where dense jungle grew on both sides of the road. Instructions were given for the withdrawal of the III Indian Corps, leaving the Japanese unchallenged for 30 miles. Bridges along the road were to be left intact "to give the impression of a helter-skelter retreat and tempt the Japanese to become over-confident and careless as they continued their advance".[5]

The 2/30th was ordered to act as a "shock-absorber" at first contact with the enemy. They were directed to inflict as many casualties as possible and to hold their position for at least 24 hours before falling back. B Company, commanded by Captain Jack Duffy, was tasked with springing the ambush while the rest of the battalion took other positions around Gemas. At around 4pm on 14 January a small number of Japanese soldiers on bicycles reached the ambush site, followed by a column of Japanese troops riding five or six abreast. Duffy decided to allow the 200 to 300 cyclists through to be dealt with by the troops in the rear. The first group was followed by several hundred more Japanese on bicycles, led by three motorcyclists. As soon as this second group was tightly packed into the ambush site and on the bridge, Duffy gave the order to blow the bridge.

One of the gunners from 2/15 Field Regiment would describe the spectacle:

> With a roar like the crack of doom, the bridge and the Japanese on it soared skywards on a dense column of smoke and fragments. This was the signal for hellfire to break out. From each side of the road for a length of half a mile the Aussies poured into the congested, panic-stricken ranks of Japanese cyclists a devastating fire with machine guns, sub-machine guns and rifles; while our men leisurely removed pins from Mills grenades and rolled them over the lip of the defile to further rend the enemy ranks with their ear-splitting bursts.[6]

Within 20 minutes the battle was over and "the entire 300 yards of road was thickly covered with dead and dying men," as Duffy reported. He then ordered his men to withdraw through the jungle where they had to fight their way out through surrounding Japanese forces, suffering a number of casualties.

Despite the resounding success of the ambush, within six hours the Japanese had rebuilt the bridge and resumed the advance with their tanks moving towards the battalion's main position, a roadblock just outside Gemas. Soon after 9am on 15 January, six of the eight tanks that advanced on the roadblock were destroyed by the soldiers of C Company. As the first members of Captain Duffy's company reached the main force with news of their successful ambush, Colonel Galleghan ordered D Company to advance on a hill held by the Japanese, inflicting heavy casualties and forcing the enemy to withdraw. The company continued their attack, despite Japanese resistance, until they were confronted by several tanks and came under heavy crossfire that forced them to pull back. Japanese dive-bombers then began hitting Gemas and the battalion headquarters where no trenches had been dug and the men were hopelessly exposed. As increasing numbers of Japanese troops began to surge into the area, by early afternoon the battalion was forced to withdraw.

Over two days of intense fighting the 2/30th Battalion had lost about 20 men and seen another 50 wounded but the Japanese had suffered the worst setback since their invasion began, with the estimated loss of 1000 men. Shocked by the tactical skill and determination of the Australian troops, Colonel Masanobu Tsuji would later concede that the Australians had fought "with a bravery we had not previously seen". When news of the action reached Australia, *The Argus* newspaper credited General Bennett with creating "from the raw material of the 8th Division the most deadly jungle fighters in the world". For his inspired leadership at Gemas, Black Jack Galleghan would be awarded the Distinguished Service Order and be lauded as a new hero of the AIF. But the Australian public's elation would be short lived. Gemas would soon prove to be little more than a momentary hitch in the inexorable, unstoppable advance of the Japanese army towards the prize of Singapore.

As the Battle of Gemas entered its final stages, a large Japanese force crossed the Muar River about 50 miles south of Gemas, flanking the coastal township and the Indian garrison's only reserve battalion. By nightfall on 16 January, despite fierce resistance by Australian artillery, Muar and its harbour had fallen to the Japanese. The following days, as the Japanese pushed forward, would see some of the bloodiest and costly fighting of the campaign – for both sides. As the Japanese attacked the settlement of Bakri, west of Muar, on 18 January, all nine of the Ha-Go light tanks spearheading the assault were destroyed by gunners from the 2/4th Australian Anti-Tank Regiment. But there were also heavy Australian casualties, with the 2/29 Battalion commander, Lieutenant Colonel John Robertson, shot dead while retreating from an attack on a Japanese roadblock. Two days later, Brigadier Herbert Duncan, commander of the 45th Indian Infantry Brigade, was also killed. With the loss of the two senior officers, command of all Allied troops around Bakri was assumed by a middle-aged, bespectacled Australian officer who would soon seize a place in Australian military folklore.

Charles Grove Wright Anderson was born in Cape Town and had served as a lieutenant with the King's African Rifles in World War I, winning the Military Cross while fighting German colonial forces in the East African campaign. After marrying an Australian, he migrated to South Australia in 1934 and became a grazier. Now the 45-year-old lieutenant colonel and commander of the 2/19 Battalion was on the front line of the desperate struggle to slow the relentless Japanese advance to Singapore.

Ordered to pull out from Bakri and attempt to break through to a nearby area where the 6th Norfolk Battalion was under intense attack, Anderson's beleaguered force was held up by a Japanese roadblock. After several failed attempts to dislodge the enemy, Anderson led a bayonet charge that broke through, personally knocking out two critical Japanese machine-gun posts with grenades. "I had an affection for grenades from the 1914–18 war and always carried two," he would later remark.[7] Over several more days of intense fighting, there were further exemplary acts of courage by Anderson before he was forced to retreat with the remnants of his force. He was later recommended for the Victoria Cross by General Bennett. The award citation would declare: "Throughout the fighting, which lasted for four days, he set a magnificent example of brave leadership, determination and outstanding courage. He not only showed fighting qualities of very high order but throughout exposed himself to danger without any regard for his own personal safety." Anderson would be the only Australian to win the VC during the Malayan campaign and remains the most senior Australian soldier to be awarded Britain's highest honour for valour.

The men under Anderson's command also fought with remarkable tenacity in hand-to-hand combat with the Japanese. Des Mulcahy, then an acting sergeant with the 2/19th, recalled several platoons responding to intense enemy sniping from a ridge. The fighting ended with what Mulcahy would describe as "a slaughter"; 55 dead Japanese. Later he went back to check the pockets of the dead Japanese to see if he could gather any useful intelligence material, and almost joined the casualty list.

After laying down his rifle, Mulcahy moved to roll over the body of the well-built Japanese who sprang to his feet holding a grenade in his right hand. His mind working "at a million miles an hour", Mulcahy immediately grabbed the soldier's left hand to stop him pulling the pin out of the grenade in his other hand. A fierce wrestling match then ensued between the two big men as Mulcahy yelled out for help from some of his mates standing 20 yards away. Frank Thomson, a gunner with the 2/4th Anti-Tank Regiment, came running across and bayoneted the Japanese through the ribs before shooting him dead. "After that, I never turned a Jap over unless it was with a bayonet," Mulcahy would later lament.[8]

As the fighting raged on the west coast, the second prong of the Japanese thrust towards Singapore was advancing on the east coast. The Japanese regiment which had landed at Kuantan in late December had moved south along jungle tracks and on 14 January the first of them – a detachment of 30 soldiers oddly decked out in black coats and khaki shorts and wearing steel helmets – were sighted by an Australian reconnaissance patrol, 15 miles north of Endau. The war was about reach Doug Lush and the signallers of his J Section at Mersing.

After two days of bombing, Endau was attacked by Japanese infantry on 18 January. Three days later, the 2/20th Battalion and 2/10 Field Regiment were in action at Mersing where they inflicted heavy casualties on the advancing enemy. But with the Japanese domination of the air smoothing the way for their ground forces – and in light of the grim news from the west – it was decided to abandon the defensive positions at Mersing and pull back to Jemaluang, about 25 miles to the south – the junction between the main roads leading to the west and down to Singapore. As the withdrawal got under way, the 2/18th Battalion mounted an ambush against a battalion-sized Japanese force on 26 January from a rubber plantation north of the Jemaluang junction. Despite the loss of 90 men killed, wounded and missing, the operation inflicted heavy casualties on the Japanese and succeeded in slowing their advance for two days. The work of the signallers from E Section and Doug Lush's J Section in the face of sustained air attacks during this period was singled out for praise by the commanders. "In the steady and orderly withdrawal in the face of a strong and triumphant enemy, daily growing in numbers and with increasing air support, our troops performed magnificently," the regimental history would record. "No small measure of the success is due to the control which commanders were able to exercise at all times, and this was made possible by a reliable Signal system."[9]

On 25 January, after a conference with senior commanders, General Percival issued the first orders for his army to begin withdrawing to Singapore island. The evacuation of the mainland was to be completed by the night of 31 January/1 February. A bridgehead force to shield the retreating troops was formed under the command of Brigadier Taylor with his 22nd Brigade battalions and various British units including the 2nd Gordon Highlanders. The signals work of the force was assigned to J Section and E Section with support from 3rd Corps Signals.

As he prepared to withdraw to his new headquarters on the island, General Bennett was engulfed by melancholy: "I toured slowly through Johore Bahru, past derelict cars and destroyed houses and the bomb holes that were everywhere. There was a deathly silence. There was not the usual crowd of chattering Malays and busy Chinese. The streets were deserted. It was a funeral march. I have never felt so sad and upset. Words fail me. This defeat should not have been."[10]

Before evacuating their base camp at Johore Bahru, the Signals units burned the attap (palm-thatch) huts that had been their temporary home. By the early hours of 31 January all of the Signals equipment had been safely moved across the strait and on to Singapore island. The Australians and the Gordons manning General Bennett's outer bridgehead moved off that night. The last to leave were the men of the 2nd Battalion Argyll and Sutherland Highlanders, who had formed an inner bridgehead. The Argylls had been in the thick of some of the heaviest fighting down the peninsula over the preceding weeks and their number had been reduced to just 90 men. But they departed the mainland in style early on the morning of 1 February, watched by the Scottish journalist and novelist Eric Linklater: "Their pipers played their own regiment out of Malaya. The morning sun was already hot when the still air was broken by 'A Hundred Pipers' and 'Heilan' Laddie' and the … Highlanders, with steady bearing and their heads high, marched from a lost campaign into a doomed island."[11]

The last of them to make the crossing was the Argylls' commanding officer, Colonel Ian Stewart, with his batman Drummer Hardy and his pet dog on a leash. Accompanying them were Doug Lush and the men from J Section who had formed the last Signals unit deployed on the mainland. Lloyd Ellerman's truck and wireless set had until the last moment held a position on the high ground on the Johore side of the Causeway in case of the need to send final messages. A small boat had been positioned nearby in the event that he had been required to run for it.[12]

In the final moments, a wave of 27 Japanese planes dropped about 50 bombs on the retreating troops. When Colonel Stewart and Lieutenant Lush reached the island side of the Causeway, the Japanese shelling suddenly intensified and most of the troops dived for cover in slit trenches. Ignoring the danger, Stewart stepped forward to be greeted by Brigadier Harold Taylor of the Australian 22nd Brigade, to Lush's astonishment: "Colonel Stewart saluted and simply said, 'Good morning, Brigadier'. The Brigadier returned the salute, both of them standing to attention in the midst of the shelling."[13]

At 8am, after the last of the men had crossed, depth-charges laid along a 25-yard section of the Causeway were detonated. The ferocious explosion sent a column of debris flying into the air and water coursing through the gap. With the severing of the last physical link to the mainland, 'Fortress Singapore' was now alone to face its fate.

Chapter 4

CAPTURED

So now the army was back on the island. It was the same
sensation as after Dunkirk. We knew where we were.
There could be no more retreat without calamity.
But driving along the north shore that morning,
back to the naval base, now an empty settlement,
I doubted for the first time that Singapore
was impregnable.

Lieutenant Commander J.O.C. Hayes, Royal Navy[1]

In the space of just eight weeks, the Japanese army had swept aside almost one and a half centuries of British hegemony in Malaya, driving the combined British, Indian and Australian force 500 miles down the Malayan peninsula and into a state of siege on Singapore island. The triumphant Lieutenant General Yamashita now installed himself in the Sultan's palace at Johore Bahru. From a glass-domed observation tower, he surveyed his trapped quarry with a powerful telescope while plotting their final defeat. The great British naval base "lay beneath one's eyes", and Tengah airfield "appeared as if it could be grasped in the hand," his intelligence officer, Colonel Tsuji, observed.

> The fight for Singapore is now on. This first class modern fort-
> ress, flaunting its impregnability, appears undaunted before our
> tired eyes. Johore Strait is over 1500 metres wide at high tide.

33

The Seletar Naval Base protects its left front, and enemy fighter planes are continuously patrolling over the straits. From various places in the rubber jungle rise columns of dense black smoke. The enemy have nearly 1000 guns large and small, and an unlimited ammunition supply – all awaiting our attack. Their anti-aircraft guns hold our aeroplanes in check with dense barrages. We know however that in the rear of the fortress the defences are weakest and we must exhaust every means in our power, whether by the plan of the gods or the plan of the devils, to reduce this great fortress by 11th February, the anniversary of the coronation of the Emperor Jimmu Tenno.[2]

The two months of fighting had exacted a terrible toll. The Allies had suffered more than 10,000 casualties – killed, wounded or missing in action. There were almost 8000 Japanese casualties. Many more were to perish on both sides in the days ahead but General Yamashita chose to pause for a week after seizing Johore to regroup and refine his plans for the Battle of Singapore. Inexplicably, and to the disgust of Doug Lush and many more of the Australians, no attempt was made to shell Yamashita in his palatial redoubt.

Sergeant Des Mulcahy railed against what he claimed were orders preventing the Australians from shelling Yamashita's observation post "because they were keeping in good with the old bloke from the palace". The Japanese had installed giant binoculars, five yards wide at the top, which were able to scan the entire panorama of Singapore: "They could see every move we made. They could see every machine gun post, everything. They could see where every Australian was before the war started."[3]

During a visit to Singapore on 20 January 1942, General Sir Archibald Wavell, the commander-in-chief of Allied forces in the south-west Pacific, had been convinced that the Japanese would launch their invasion along the north-west coast of the island. The Johore Strait was narrowest in this sector and a number of river mouths on the mainland side provided potential cover for launching amphibious landing craft. Wavell believed this would be the place to deploy the freshest and strongest troops, the British 18th Division, most of whom had arrived on 29 January. Percival strongly disagreed. He thought the attack was most likely to come down the Johore River and on the eastern side of the island. In the end, despite Wavell's growing concern that Percival was not the "really vigorous, ruthless personality" needed to organise the defence of Singapore, Percival prevailed. It would be a fateful decision for the island – and for the men of Australia's 22nd Brigade and their Signals sections.

Percival ordered the Australian 22nd and 27th Brigades to deploy along the north-west coast and sent the 18th Division and the best of the remaining Indian troops to the north-east. Brigadier Taylor and his 22nd Brigade troops – who were deployed to the westernmost sector – faced a massive challenge with severely limited resources. Their task was to defend an eight-mile front with just three battalions – half the number of men deployed along an eight-mile section of coastline near Changi on the island's north-east coast. The terrain was largely mangrove swamp and mud flats that were an operational nightmare. One officer with the 2/19 Battalion would complain that he and his men had been "dumped in a scraggy waste of stunted rubber and tangled undergrowth, apparently miles from anywhere, our vision limited to the next rise in the undulating ground and our means of movement confined to a few native foot tracks winding through the wilderness".[4] Lieutenant Frank Gaven of the 2/20th Battalion was appalled the sight: "I have never felt such a feeling of desperation in all my life. I then realised that forward defence in this situation was an impossible task."[5]

As Wavell predicted, it was from the west that the onslaught came. At dawn on 8 February, the Japanese launched a severe bombardment of Singapore and heavy artillery attacks on the areas held by the Australian brigades. At first the shelling of the western sector was considered to be either a feint or merely part of a general 'softening up' operation. But as the attack intensified through the day it became obvious that the Japanese had indeed chosen to launch the battle for Singapore from the west. It was the Australians' first experience of heavy shellfire and many were shocked and traumatised by the ordeal. The 2/18 Battalion commander Lieutenant Colonel Arthur Varley, who had endured the German shelling of Pozieres in 1916, said he had never experienced "such concentrated shellfire over such a period" in the four years of World War I. General Bennett, whose headquarters had been targeted during the morning, visited Taylor and found him "somewhat shaken". Taylor had reason to be agitated. His desperate efforts to call in artillery support for his brigade had been rebuffed and his superiors had not assembled reserves behind his men or prepared a reserve line.

The Japanese struck just after 10.30pm. The first men from a force of 16 battalions boarded a flotilla of motorboats, many towing rafts, and raced towards the positions held by the 2/18th and 2/20th battalions. The Australians responded with intense fire from their Vickers machine guns and a barrage of grenades but were soon overwhelmed. The 2/20th alone would lose more than 400 men as the waves of landing Japanese surged over and around them. Throughout the night and through the following day Taylor's brigade was pushed back as the Japanese captured their initial objective, Tengah airfield.

Around 9am on 9 February a second Japanese force came ashore in the area between the Johore Causeway and the Kranji River held by

Brigadier Duncan Maxwell's 27th Brigade. The brigade fell back after huge oil storage tanks near the causeway were blown up, sending more than nine million litres of burning oil flooding across the strait. But by the morning of 10 February the Japanese were comfortably ashore and had most of north-west Singapore under their control.

Throughout the first days of the fighting on the island, Lieutenant Doug Lush, who had been detached to work as 22nd Brigade Signals Officer, worked alongside Brigadier Taylor. Lush was responsible for keeping Taylor in touch with the various units under his brigade command. It was a challenging task. The preliminary bombardment by the Japanese had severed most of the telephone lines running to the companies on the front lines. And the brigade's wireless sets had only returned from servicing the morning of the Japanese landings and the smaller and less powerful battalion sets proved to be of little use. Despite these setbacks, the signallers worked feverishly to maintain communications. Lieutenant Colonel Roland Oakes would later write: "From the shelter of a slit trench in which I was crouching, I saw a regimental signaller lying in the open nearby, in the middle of a severe shelling bout, transmitting messages on a line phone he had connected up. And this was typical of the whole tribe throughout the campaign."[6]

On the afternoon of 9 February the decision was made to relocate Taylor's headquarters from Bukit Timah to Holland Road, several miles closer to the centre of the city. A night of hectic activity followed as the Signals team packed up the large quantities of stores and equipment. In the early hours of the morning, the Japanese began shelling and bombing the area and several quartermaster staff who were among the last to leave narrowly escaped being hit. The teams immediately began work laying cable from their new Holland Road office, led by Doug Lush.

The new brigade headquarters was a grand colonial villa with a spacious entrance, extensive gardens and a driveway that suited the requirements for the brigade's vehicles. At the rear of the house was a locked storeroom beside a recently dug large trench. From their Signals Office in one of the outbuildings, Lush's team sought to re-establish communications with the three infantry Battalions – 2/18th, 2/19th and 2/20th – and Divisional headquarters.

The Australians soon discovered that the house previously had been occupied by a Doctor Duke. The doctor's belongings, including furnishings, personal effects and even clothing, had been left behind when he hastily departed. Lush, who had lost much of his kit during the final days of fighting on the Malay Peninsula, found some handy items including a pair of golf shoes to replace the gumboots he'd been wearing for a week after losing his army boots.

The signallers increasingly were being called on to fight as well as maintain the brigade's precarious communications. Just before the move to Holland Road, on 11 February, several signallers from Lush's cable party were involved in a desperate effort to silence a menacing Japanese machine gun located near their headquarters. The Brigade Major, Major Rex Beale, had ordered several of the signallers to arm themselves with grenades and join him in an attack on the machine gun position. As they made their way forward, one of the signallers, Lance Sergeant Geoff Bingham – who would be awarded the Military Medal for his bravery during the Singapore fighting – was hit and had to be carried away by Signaller Todd Morgan.

Major Beale was also hit in the hip and Lance Corporal Bobby Hook, a signaller from Donald in Victoria, was wounded in the chest. Despite his own injury, Morgan picked up Hook and carried him back to the unit's position. After the fighting ended, Beale and Hook were conveyed to the Alexandria Hospital, where Hook died of his wounds and Beale was executed after the Japanese captured the hospital a few days later. Bingham was luckier. He was instead taken to St Andrew's Cathedral, which was being used as a main medical post, and would recover from his wounds.

Shortly after this incident, Lush was ordered by Brigadier Taylor to investigate the Signals position to the brigade's rear on Reformatory Road, several miles from the new Holland Road headquarters. The Japanese had captured a section of the road following a skirmish with Australian troops. After completing his task in the early evening, Lush began heading back to Holland Road with Captain John Paterson and stumbled into another serious fight. The Japanese had driven three ammunition trucks captured from the 2/18th Battalion into an Australian ambush. As the Australians opened fire, killing all three drivers, the trucks exploded with tremendous force.

In the final days of the Battle of Singapore, the Japanese were held to a tenuous perimeter that ran close to the Holland Road villa. The men of the 22nd Brigade headquarters were subjected to intermittent mortar bombardment and ran out of water. One day, as the Japanese bombing continued, one of Lush's Signals staff broke into the locked storeroom at the back of the house to discover it was stacked full of canned food. The timing was fortuitous. The unit's rations had run out and the men had been without food for a couple of days. "What a relief to find this food on hand," Lush would recall. "We found the storeroom was full of sardines and green peas, and so for the next couple of days we had sardines and green peas for breakfast, sardines and green peas for lunch and sardines and green peas for dinner."

By 12 February the situation in Singapore was rapidly deteriorating. The 22nd Brigade could muster only 800 men from the three infantry battalions and machine gun battalion that had started the battle with roughly 3400 men. Two days later, the 2/4th Machine Gun Battalion's commander, Lieutenant Colonel Michael Anketell, was mortally wounded. After Harold Taylor collapsed from exhaustion and was hospitalised, Lieutenant Colonel Arthur Varley was promoted to command the 22nd Brigade.

Varley had distinguished himself during World War I. He won the Military Cross for his gallantry during the battle of Messines in June 1917 and a second award bar to the decoration for his bravery supplying forward positions under artillery fire in August 1918. The new brigadier and several of his senior staff were just beginning to settle themselves in Doctor Duke's villa when word came through that General Percival had agreed to an unconditional surrender with the Japanese.

The Allied troops faced an impossible situation after the Japanese captured the MacRitchie Reservoir and water became in desperately short supply for both the civilian population and those many wounded now being cared for in various hospitals. General Percival was left with no choice. He sent his last telegram to Wavell on 15 February: "Owing to losses from enemy action, water, petrol, food and ammunition practically finished. Unable therefore to continue the fight any longer. All ranks have done their best and are grateful for your help."

Late that afternoon, Perceval drove with a sombre posse of senior officers to the shell-damaged Ford Motor Factory near Bukit Timah village where, after a brief and terse meeting with General Yamashita, he signed the document of surrender at 7.50pm. As Mark Clisby would write: "With the signing of these terms of surrender, 100,000 Allied soldiers, including nearly 15,000 Australians, would be led into captivity. After only eight weeks of fighting, the Japanese were the undisputed masters of Singapore and the entire Malayan Peninsula."[7]

As the haunting silence of surrender spread across the city, uncertainty and apprehension took hold among the defeated army. At Holland Road, Doug Lush and his men fearfully pondered what fate had next in store for them: "So the war for us was now over – and what a disaster. What was now to become of us?"

In the absence of any further news and anxious to find out what was going on, Lush decided to visit the 8th Division headquarters at Tanglin Barracks. Accompanying him on the short drive was Captain Bill Bathgate, another member of the brigade staff. They arrived at the barracks to find that confusion reigned. Amidst a huddle of senior officers, the Australian commander, General Bennett, was in deep and tense conversation with Colonel Jim Thyer, one of Bennett's most senior aides and former CO of the 8th Division Signals. Unable to learn anything, Lush and Bathgate soon headed back to the villa.

After a brief discussion between Lush, Bathgate and Lieutenant Ralph Johnson, another Brigade staff officer, they resolved to approach Brigadier Varley to discuss the possibility of an escape. It was around 8pm when they met. The men outlined their plan to flee north through Malaya and Thailand to try to reach the British lines in Burma. Varley was abrupt and adamant in his dismissal of the proposal, despite agreeing with the principle that it was the duty of every officer to try to escape. He ordered each of the officers to remain with their men and accept the surrender.

The young officers would soon be astonished by the news that Major General Bennett, along with a small group of his staff, had defied his own orders and escaped, eventually making his way back to Australia. Despite his disappointment at being denied the possibility of escaping himself, Lush for one would side with Bennett's later highly controversial decision to abandon Singapore and his army. "It's everyone's duty not just an officer's duty to not get caught, and if you are caught you've got to try to escape," he would later say. "The point is the Australians did not surrender on Singapore; it was Percival who had capitulated." The competitive athlete in Lush lamented the failure of the campaign: "When you fight you must fight to win and not all of us in the military and the civil administration had fought all out to win."

Like all of the Australian units scattered across Singapore island, the 22nd Brigade headquarters staff were instructed to remain at their locations, lay down all their arms and equipment and await further instructions. Lush ordered his men to throw away the bolts from their rifles and to sabotage as much of their equipment as possible. Screwdrivers were used to bend the relays at the back of the switchboards to make them unusable. All telephones were rendered inoperable by throwing away the microphones and all the telephone operating equipment was destroyed. When Japanese troops began moving through the area collecting vehicles, a couple of days after the surrender, they were thwarted on arrival at Doctor Duke's house to discover that all the ignition keys and steering lock keys were missing. "I suppose I could have been shot for that," Lush would say.

At 11am on 18 February, Lush and his men were instructed to assemble outside the house on Holland Road with all their belongings. They were now formally prisoners of war. It was soon confirmed that they were all under orders to march to an undisclosed location. They did not know until later in the day, but that destination was Changi, on the eastern edge of the island, which had been a barracks for many of the troops earlier in the war. As they prepared to move off, Doug Lush put on Doctor Duke's golf shoes which would serve him well on the 19-mile march to their prison.

The Japanese had issued clear instructions that the prisoners were to leave behind all vehicles. At the last moment Lush felt compelled to disregard the order – with potentially disastrous consequences. About 15 minutes before they were marched out, while still assembled on the road awaiting orders, Signaller Bob Boughton approached Lush with a serious concern. Lush had earlier recruited Boughton from Brigade Headquarters as a dispatch rider as he could drive a car and also ride a motorbike. But a recent accident meant he now had difficulty walking – and a day-long march was out of the question. Lush resolved to take one of the brigade staff cars and get Boughton to drive with them to their destination. In the hope that it would add legitimacy to the act of disobedience, he ordered that the car be loaded with the remaining tinned food from Dr Duke's store. Boughton was instructed to drive slowly as the men marched and, on arrival, to unload the car, guard the food and then get rid of the car.

The march was long and exhausting in Singapore's eternal heat. The small party of signallers and Brigade headquarters staff managed to cover only about a mile every hour.

Thirst soon became a big problem as the men did not have water bottles. Chinese living along the route rushed out offering the men pannikins of water, to the annoyance of the Japanese guards who kept chasing them away. Had it not been for the courageous actions of hundreds of Chinese, many more of the marchers would have collapsed from exhaustion and dehydration.

Boughton accompanied the procession driving slowly but eventually pulled ahead, arriving at Changi several hours before the rest, who didn't reach the barracks until about 3am. Lush was one of the last officers from the brigade to reach the camp. By the time he finally arrived, the other officers were all sitting around drinking tea. After checking that his men had found a place to rest, he rustled up a mug of tea for himself. As soon as he removed his shoes and wrapped them in his shirt to make a pillow, he slumped onto the concrete floor and fell fast asleep.

Chapter 5

CHANGI

Alas for the prestige of the white man in the East.

Major Jim Jacobs, 8th Division Signals[1]

The white man's new burden was to be imprisoned in the military camp that had once boasted the reach of Britain's empire in the Far East – by the Asian nation that would soon usurp that colonial ascendancy across the sweep of South-East Asia. Built in 1938 as part of the Changi Garrison, the grand Selerang Barracks had been home to the 2nd Battalion of the Gordon Highlanders. It had sustained heavy damage during the final weeks of fighting – including the destruction of electrical, water and sewerage systems.

Sergeant Des Mulcahy found a scene of chaos on his arrival. Most of the buildings had suffered serious bomb damage from Japanese air and ground attacks during the final stages of the battle. On the parade ground, there were three large craters where bombs had landed but had not exploded. The unexploded ordnance would remain buried beneath the ground where the POWs would be required to parade over the coming weeks. It would take about a week after their arrival before the prisoners managed to restore the water supply. The Indian troops were then tasked with building a high wire fence around the camp.[2] Despite the damage, the barracks initially offered relatively

45

comfortable accommodation for the British and Australian prisoners confined there. That soon changed with rapidly dwindling food supplies and overcrowding.

Among the most forlorn of the new captives was General Arthur Percival. According to historian Clifford Kinvig, the defeated GOC (General Officer Commanding) could be seen sitting head in hands, outside the married quarters he now shared with seven brigadiers, a colonel, his aide-de-camp and a cook-sergeant: "He discussed his feelings with few, spent hours walking around the extensive compound, ruminating on the reverse and what might have been."[3] Along with all of the other Allied officers above the rank of colonel, Percival was soon sent to Formosa (Taiwan) and then on to Manchuria where he would be held for the duration of the war with many other VIP captives, including Major General Jonathan Wainwright, who had commanded the ill-fated American forces in the Philippines.

After the departure of Percival, leadership of the Australian prisoners passed to Colonel Wilfrid Kent Hughes, who had been assistant adjutant and quartermaster general of the 8th Division. Billy Kent Hughes had distinguished himself in World War I, being wounded while fighting with the 8th Light Horse at Gallipoli and winning the Military Cross in Palestine. Between the wars, he was a politician who gained notoriety for publicly flirting with fascism. That did not, however, hamper his political progress. After World War II, he would serve as deputy premier of Victoria before becoming a member of the federal Cabinet under Sir Robert Menzies. He would also publish one of the most eccentric accounts of the war in Asia, *Slaves of the Samurai* – 50,000 words of verse written in ink on 20 small pieces of paper that were smuggled out of Changi in a tin of talcum powder.

Kent Hughes' other great claim to fame was as a sportsman and sports bureaucrat. He had competed for Australia at the 1920 Summer Olympics and would go on to chair the organising committee for the 1956 Games in Melbourne. As a hurdler and manager of the Australian team at the 1938 Empire Games in Sydney, he was also well known to Doug Lush and Stewart Embling. On his first morning in Changi, Lush awoke to orders that he must report immediately to Kent Hughes. On this occasion, the colonel was in no mood for sporting reminiscences.

No sooner had the lieutenant presented himself than Kent Hughes barked: "Lush, did you authorise a car to come into this area?" Stunned by the news that Signalman Boughton had failed to follow orders to dispose of the car after unloading the cargo of food from Dr Duke's house, Lush replied, "Yes, sir". The colonel quickly snapped back, "Then you will take it back to where it had come from, all 19 miles and you will do it immediately!"

After locating the car, but not its driver, Lush discovered the vehicle was out of fuel. Still exhausted from the previous day's walk to the camp, he trudged over to the Australian Army Service Corps quarters where he was given two gallons of petrol. He then proceeded to drive the car back towards the city, convinced that he would never make it past the armed Japanese guards and the tanks prowling the streets. He realised he had to get rid of the car as quickly as possible. As he drove down past the Changi jail, Lush came across a Japanese soldier standing guard with his rifle and bayonet fixed.

Pulling up about 25 yards away, Lush got out of the car as the soldier came on guard. Fearing the soldier might be preparing to shoot, Lush leant back inside the car and removed the keys. With that, the soldier took a couple of steps forward with his rifle levelled. With the keys in his hand, Lush took a couple of steps forward before throwing the keys, which landed at the feet of the Japanese: "He picked up the keys and took a couple of steps towards the car. I began to walk backwards and then he got up to the car and lent through the driver's side window, I guess to see if there was a bomb or something in there. With that, I turned and quietly walked away. And that's how I got rid of the bloody car."

In the first weeks after the surrender, Lieutenant Colonel Charles Kappe, the 8th Division's Chief Signals Officer, ordered a meeting of all the unit's officers in the camp. Lush noted the irony that it had taken the Japanese victory for him and his fellow divisional Signals officers to be gathered together for the first time in one place. Kappe briefed the men on the decision to form two officers' messes. There was to be an A mess for captains and more senior officers and a B mess for lieutenants. This immediately revived a frustration for Lush. Of all the original Signals officers, he was the only one who was still a lieutenant – despite having been advised shortly before the fall of Singapore that he was to be promoted to the rank of captain. Along with his friend Lionel Matthews, who was by this time a captain, Lush was the only one of the current officers from his unit who had been in action in both Malaya and during the siege of Singapore. His mess segregation from the other experienced Signals officers reinforced his poor opinion of Kappe, who he regarded as arrogant and insensitive to the feelings of the men under him, although after the war Kappe would pen him a glowing commendation.

Soon after the prisoners' arrival at Changi, Lieutenant General Tomoyuki Yamashita decided to make a triumphal tour to inspect the human spoils of his victory. All of the British and Australian prisoners were ordered to line the camp roads in the best of the dress they still had, as Signals Major Jim Jacobs recounted:

> We were kept waiting in the hot sun for about an hour and a half, but at last Yamashita arrived. Truckloads of armed Japs in front and in rear of Yamashita's staff car formed the escort, and a long procession of captured limousines followed him. It was very galling to see the grinning yellow so and so's riding in triumph in luxury cars which had belonged to the British just a few weeks before. The 'Tiger of Malaya' was a tough looking guy and looked quite capable of the heinous crimes with which he was charged after the war and for which he paid with his life.[4]

Food shortages in the camp soon began to be felt. The senior officers decided to cut rations while most of the men remained reasonably fit and healthy. This would further expose the disparity in physical condition between those men who had been in the thick of the fighting down the Malay Peninsula and those who had remained in Singapore in administrative jobs, well fed and well provisioned.

Lush, who was in poor health and had lost some weight since arriving at the camp, met up with a former colleague from his insurance office back in Melbourne who was a captain with the 4th Motor Transport Company. The captain had arrived at Changi with a large steel trunk containing his equipment and all of his uniforms and had since acquired a proper camp bed. He gave a tin of condensed milk to Lush, who hid it under his blankets, making the secret luxury last for several days.

Time passed slowly in the camp and the men had very little to keep them occupied. One day Lush walked out to a section of the camp where a large water tower stood. After climbing up the tower, he gazed out towards the Straits of Johore where he could clearly make out what appeared to be a fleet of Japanese naval vessels, some of which were badly damaged, making their way towards the naval base. He assumed they must have been engaged with the Allied naval fleet which had just seen battle in the Coral Sea.

After about five weeks, the Japanese called for a party of prisoners to go out into Singapore to work. Two thousand prisoners formed the party, including between two and three hundred men from the 8th Division Signals. An officer was placed in charge of groups of about a hundred men. Lush volunteered to join the first main working party to leave the camp. He marched out in his prized golf shoes with a dixie of rice. As his group headed up a hill, they came to a guard post manned by a group of Sikh soldiers who had defected from the British Army and were now working as sentries for the Japanese. As the party came level with the guard post, one of the men warned Lush that he should probably give them an 'eyes right' salute, to which he replied, "I'm not going to give those bastards an eyes right!" As the Australians marched though, ignoring the Indians, there was a sudden scream and several of the Sikh guards rushed forward with fixed bayonets. Reluctantly, Lush called, "Righto fellas, give them an 'eyes right'." The guards stopped in their tracks halfway down the hill, and the party was able to march on towards the centre of Singapore island.

The local Chinese traders had heard the prisoners were coming out and they gathered along the road offering bread rolls for sale. The men who had money were delighted to buy. Some of those who didn't and were desperately hungry took matters into their own hands and snatched the rolls, forgetting the kindness so recently extended by the Chinese who gave water to those prisoners suffering on the long march into captivity at Changi.

The working party's destination, still unconfirmed as the day wore on, was a place that once was a byword for the pampered indulgence of British colonial life in Singapore. Its tarnished opulence would soon mock the sufferings of the new residents.

Chapter 6

ADAM PARK

Some say if you sit and listen you can still hear the
echoes of the battle reverberating through the very walls.
Some say you can see the ghosts of dead POWs that
flit between the evening shadows.

Jon Cooper, Tigers in the Park[1]

The Changi work party's destination was the Adam Park estate in Bukit Timah, an exclusive prewar enclave of grand black and white colonial villas set amid lush tropical gardens. The area, a few miles north-west of the central business district of Singapore below the MacRitchie Reservoir, had been the scene of some of the heaviest fighting in the final days before the fall of Singapore. Now it was the site of a new prisoner of war camp.

Groups of about 90 men were allocated to each of the 19 villas on the estate. Lush and his men were assigned to House 16. In the servants' quarters they discovered a large sack of lentils which they would devour over the following few days. With fellow officers Ken Trumble and George Mansfield, Lush took up residence in a section of the veranda. The work party was soon told that their task was to construct a roadway around the Singapore Golf Links, adjacent to the reservoir, and to build a memorial shrine for the Japanese soldiers killed during the Battle of Singapore, on the highest point in the immediate area.

Adam Park had been comprehensively looted and vandalised by local civilians after the British residents fled. All the fans had been stolen from the villas as had all the brass fittings from the doors, which the prisoners now used as firewood to cook their daily rice rations. But amid the trash there was some treasure. Soon after their arrival, Tony Burfitt, one of the electricians from Lush's J Section, discovered a radio among the discarded furniture of House 16. It was a locally produced model and was still in its cabinet housing. Burfitt removed the cabinet and soon had the radio working again. It was then concealed in the ceiling of a section of the veranda above the bed where Doug Lush slept – a wonderful, and very dangerous, asset which provided the men with daily international short-wave news reports.

The men positioned an old wardrobe against the entrance to the veranda, placed in such a way that the Japanese guards could not easily see around it. On the wall next to Lush's bed was a power point and the radio was hooked up to that: "Listening to it was no trouble at all. Each night I would just switch the power on and I had a lead coming down to just an earpiece and that used to fit into the top of the bamboo leg of my bed. I used to keep it covered over and if the Japs came in I could just quickly cover it all up. We lived with that for six months."

Had the radio been discovered, Lush and his fellow prisoners risked severe punishment, even execution. It was a risk they were willing to take to maintain a tenuous link with the world beyond their prison and particularly to track the course of the war, but the danger of discovery was constant and once their secret was almost exposed. When the men had settled down in the evenings after work, the Japanese would sometimes arrive unheralded for an inspection, suddenly appearing beside Lush's bed demanding a rollcall for the sick men who were unable to work the next day. "One night when I was relaxing in my bunk, listening to the BBC, a Japanese guard suddenly appeared at the house looking for me," Lush recalled. "He came straight around the wardrobe. At the command 'Kurrah', I immediately jumped up and made a bit of a polite fuss of this guard so as to cover up the fact that I was trying to turn the radio off as subtly as possible. It never occurred to him that there may have been a hidden radio above my bed, a highly punishable offence. Fortunately, the guard sort of melted a bit when I was being so polite to him. It greatly assisted me, so I was then able to cover up the radio's presence. But it was still a close call."

A second radio was smuggled into Adam Park by Harold Fischer, a signaller from the Melbourne suburb of Armidale. According to Lloyd Ellerman, Fischer was "one of the best and most fearless scroungers" among the Australian prisoners: "He and I were together at Adam Park, sleeping under the floor of the house which was built some five feet above the ground and it was quite a comfortable spot. Harold had acquired a six valve wireless set. We had an old ice chest between our two bunks and there was a false bottom in the chest all full of novels etcetera. Just before midnight we'd rearrange things, get out our earphones and listen to the BBC news. Despite the fact that the news was nearly all bad, we enjoyed listening and right in front of the Japanese."[2]

Apart from tasks assigned to specialists such as the electricians, the rest of the prisoners were detailed to work each day on the golf links road and the shrine. Those on the work parties were paid in Japanese wartime paper currency – 10 cents per day each, 15 cents for sergeants and 25 cents for officers. Those who didn't work got nothing. Each morning and night there would be a rollcall parade to organise the work parties. The sergeants and corporals were required to give a report of everyone attending the parade to the officers. In the mornings the men would assemble on the roadway and march to the golf links where the Japanese engineers would allocate work to be done in various areas. At lunchtime a large kerosene tin of hot water was provided, into which the men would dive their mugs or empty Spam tins.

It was arduous work in the relentless heat and humidity of the tropics and the guards drove the men hard. If the crews slowed down or took an unauthorised break, they would be ordered to work harder – "Speedo, Speedo" – often accompanied by a beating. Once Lush counselled the men, "Take it easy fellas, we can't work like this for too long in the full heat of the day." His disobedience soon drew the ire of the Japanese, and the first of many violent assaults he would endure as a prisoner of war: "A Japanese engineer came up to me and said that I was a bad officer and a bad influence on the men. He then hit me on the head with a hammer with not a lot of force, fortunately, over my hat. But I still sagged at the knees when he struck me. I looked at him and said, 'You bastard', but we quickly learnt that if you showed any fight they would give you a really good belting, so you really just had to take it and grin and bear it."

The men were given only rudimentary tools to work with. The road crews mostly were issued with chunkels – rough, wide-headed gardening hoes. At the end of the day's work, some of the men would throw their chunkels into the lake. The Japanese realised the tools were going missing but did now know how. Their response was to offer the prisoners two Singapore dollars at the end of each day when the chunkels were returned. Suddenly, all of the tools thrown into the lake reappeared.

The hardships the men suffered in the Singapore work camps were a mild foretaste of what lay ahead for many of them. "The Japanese guards stood over us every day but it was a piece of cake compared with what would happen on the Thai–Burma railway later on," Lush would later recall. "The moment you moved away from Singapore island it changed. The real hardship was going to a foreign country where you were not familiar with things and had to make your own way. Those that remained in Changi had it far easier. They did not have that much contact with the Japanese. It was the poor buggers that were sent out from Singapore that had the worst time."

Because of the extent of the damage done to houses and other buildings around Adam Park during the final weeks of fighting, the Japanese had to call on electricians and other technicians among their prisoners to restore power supply. Lieutenant George Mansfield was placed in charge of a group of workers who went out each day restoring power and light in the Adam Park area. Some of Lush's men who formed these working parties were very skilled electricians and their work was greatly valued by the Japanese guards, who fed and treated them better than the other prisoners. But with hundreds of other men over-worked, under-fed and forced to live in cramped conditions, morale soon became a serious problem that needed to be addressed by the officers.

When the men came home each night after a long day's work, they were tired and irritable. They would lie about with nothing to occupy themselves with except talk about food and work and when they would be going home. Lush thought that if he could obtain some books it might help to overcome the men's boredom.

One morning, after the men had lined up on parade and moved off to their work sites, Lush borrowed a Japanese electrician's armband from one of the men. He invited Signalman Keith Martin, who was on sick leave that day, to accompany him. The pair then walked together past the Japanese house guard giving a "very fine" salute and then crossed Bukit Timah Road and headed to Farrar Road, where there were a number of beautiful villas that were now abandoned. Selecting one villa that was set back behind a long driveway, Lush suggested to Martin that he should wait hidden in the hedgerow that divided the house from the adjoining property while he made a reconnaissance.

Lush entered the house through an imposing entrance that opened onto a large black and white tiled reception area. During a quick inspection of the premises, he discovered a bookcase to the rear of a hallway. On opening the glass doors, he found a large assortment of books. He immediately began making a selection that he placed in piles on the floor. It was then that he suddenly noticed a Japanese staff car approaching the house. Fearing the worst, he jumped up and rushed back to the entrance where he seized hold of an electric cable hanging from where a large fan had been removed from the centre of the ceiling in the reception area.

Moments later, two Japanese officers strode into the house and confronted Lush. One of them angrily shouted, "Kurrah!" ("Hey you!") and with that the other officer approached and struck the prisoner across the head. Indignantly pointing to his armband, Lush declared, "I am an electrician". This temporarily eased the situation. While their driver stood guard, the officers made a quick inspection of the house and, not noticing the pile of books in the hallway, seemed satisfied there was nothing out of order. While he stood, still clutching the wire, the officers struck Lush across the head once again and then ordered him to go.

As he slowly walked away down the driveway, Lush gave a furtive signal to Martin, now squatting in the hedgerow, to be quiet while the staff car followed him out into the street. As he began to walk back towards their camp, the car moved off. Once it was out of sight,

Lush retraced his steps to where Martin was still waiting. They then moved back into the house to retrieve their haul.

With 40 to 50 books selected, the problem was how to carry them. After a further search of the house, Lush found a large black leather suitcase into which he and Martin loaded their haul. As they struggled back down the road with the heavy case, the pair noticed, leaning against the fence, a bicycle with a carrier basket attached. They hauled the load of books onto the bike and wheeled their way back to the camp, once again saluting the guard on their arrival. That night, Lush took great pleasure in distributing the books among the men, who were thrilled. These books were read over and over again and were later carried by the men to the work camps beyond Singapore where they would spend the rest of the war.

Years after the war ended, when Lush and his wife were moving into their new home in Melbourne, his kitbag was rediscovered. On opening the bag, he found two books that brought back mixed memories. They were *The King's Grace* by John Buchan and *Modern Ski-ing* by A.H. D'Egville. The flyleaf of both books was signed "Lillian Gibson of Cluny, Singapore". The Lushes resolved to call their new house 'Cluny' and that name in brass letters adorned the entrance to the property for the rest of their lives. The Cluny Park estate would find new fame as one of the extravagant locations in the 2018 movie *Crazy Rich Asians*.

Beyond the respite provided by the sudden acquisition of a stolen library, the prisoners needed to be creative in developing recreational activities to ease the burden of their lives in captivity. One of the more inventive diversions was staged to celebrate Melbourne Cup Day on 3 November 1942. As no horses were available, it was decided frogs could be 'raced' instead. A number of the camp punters constructed a frog-racing arena on one of the lawn tennis courts adjoining the houses. The arena consisted of an enclosed circle about seven yards in diameter. In the middle was placed a box tied by string that stretched across the arena from side to side. Just before the event started, the frogs were placed together under the box. Once the starter pulled the string, the box lifted and the frogs were free to hop out. The one that jumped out of the arena first would be declared the winner. Many frogs were recruited and trained ahead of the big day, all were named and some given pedigrees, such as "Gordon Bennett, out of Singapore by Capitulation".[3]

The Melbourne Cup 'hop', with a big field of frog entrants, proved to be a breathtaking event. A big bullfrog named 'Triggerman', owned and trained by Captain William Dixon, waited after the box was lifted and all the other frogs had started to hop away. Dixon's bullfrog then took one giant leap from a standing start and cleared the arena perimeter. He was cheered as the winner and the 'Melbourne Cup' was presented to Dixon. The trophy had been constructed by one of the prisoners from two inverted halves of a large coconut joined together with some scrap metal salvaged from around the camp. It was brought back to Melbourne after the war and proudly displayed in the Preston Motors showroom where Dixon worked. Later it was donated to the Australian War Memorial, where it went on public display.

Around this time, Lush discovered some of the men were engaged in a highly risky racket selling petrol to the local Chinese. At a large, burnt-out petrol dump located beside a nearby racecourse, the men had discovered 44-gallon drums still containing small quantities of petrol that they were collecting to furtively sell to the local businessmen.

After rollcall one night, Lush decided to visit the area accompanied by one of the men involved. They went over the wire fence surrounding the camp, successfully dodging the mobile guards. When they reached the dump, several men could be seen emptying the residue from multiple drums of petrol into another drum, sealing it and then rolling it to a spot in the long grass at the edge of the adjoining road. Each night the men aimed to fill one or two drums and negotiate their sale to locals at a secluded spot by the road. Realising the severe punishments likely if the Japanese discovered the operation – a risk heightened by the 'frightful' racket raised by the drums being rolled down the road at midnight – Lush ordered a halt to it.

Another inventive petrol racket involved members of the Adam Park road-working party. The steamroller driver was Signaller Bob Bedford. Each day Bedford would approach the Japanese authorities for a ration of petrol for his machine – a quite audacious scam given that the steamroller was not powered by gasoline. In their ignorance, the guards duly issued Bedford with the petrol which each afternoon he would sell on the thriving Chinese black market.

After about eight months, the work on the shrine and the road around the MacRitchie Reservoir was almost finished. The Adam Park prisoners were then informed that a 'special work party' was to be formed from among them and they would shortly be departing Singapore to an unspecified destination.

Signaller Jack Chapman remembers the day – 23 November 1942 – as it was the birthday of his younger brother, Colin. "It was explained to us that the new work camp and the area in question were 'like holiday Pacific island, prenty food'," Chapman recalled. "We knew that almost every Allied plisoner – oops, prisoner! – on Singapore island would eventually be drafted to one work party or another … so our little lot decided to go and enjoy the holiday resort together."[4]

Within a few days, the journey began. Soon after a large group of the men at Adam Park had been selected, they were moved to the nearby Sime Road Camp where a medical inspection was conducted. According to Lush, this included the 'glass rod' anal inspection test, so the Japanese could eliminate those deemed to be diseased. From Sime Road the prisoners were bussed to Singapore Harbour.

Before the men billeted at House 16 Adam Park left, a priority was to pack their precious secret radio to bring with them. The radio was dismantled by the electricians and the parts concealed in five water bottles. The sides of each of the water bottles were opened out and then covered over again once the radio parts were safely fitted inside. Then disaster struck. The water bottle containing a couple of the radio's valves was dropped and the valves broken. The radio was now useless and had to be abandoned.

The departure from Singapore would be a wrenching, and sometimes permanent, separation for men who had formed close bonds fighting together and sharing their captivity for more than a year. It would break up the small, close-knit group that Doug Lush had led, among them electricians Bill Constable and Tony Burfitt. Constable was later sent with the work force to Borneo, where he died at Sandakan in May 1945. Burfitt was sent to work on the infamous Thai–Burma railway but would survive the war.

Many other Australian prisoners had left Singapore well before the men from Adam Park. The first 3000 Australians deployed to work on the Thai–Burma railway had left Changi in May 1942. In July, another 1500 from Changi were selected to be sent to Sandakan – a name that would soon become as notorious as the railway as a place of death and depravity. Among the 10 Signals officers sent to Borneo with 'B Force' was one whose selfless bravery – and shocking death – would come to exemplify the finest defiant spirit of the captured Australians.

Lionel Matthews was born in Adelaide, but enlisted with Signals in Melbourne and arrived for initial training at the Casula camp in Sydney on the same day in July 1940 as Doug Lush, who became a firm friend. Matthews was awarded the Military Cross for his courage maintaining cable communications under heavy fire during the spectacular ambush of the advancing Japanese at Gemas in January 1942 and again during the final days of fighting in Singapore. But he would display even greater bravery as a prisoner in Borneo.

From the Sandakan POW camp, Matthews personally built and directed an underground intelligence organisation. He arranged through native contacts for the delivery of desperately needed medicines, food and money to the camp. He scrounged parts to build a secret radio link with the outside world, arranged escape parties and negotiated the delivery of a cache of firearms as he plotted an uprising against the Japanese in partnership with guerrilla forces in the southern Philippines. But his luck ran out in July 1944 when the *Kempeitai*, the Japanese military police, made a surprise raid on the camp and uncovered some arms, maps and diaries.

After enduring months of torture and interrogation, Captain Matthews was hauled before a kangaroo court that ordered his summary execution on 2 March 1944, as fellow Signals officer Jim Hardacre would recount: "Normally execution is carried out with the ceremonial sword, but the Japanese in their Bushido Code considered Matthews a very brave man, giving him the choice between the sword beheading or the firing squad; naturally he opted for the British way. Outside the court he saw the six-man execution squad of Jap soldiers. Spurning the blindfold, he awaited the end, no doubt with a prayer on his lips. As shots rang out he slumped to the ground. Death was instantaneous."[5]

Lionel Matthews was posthumously awarded the George Cross, the second highest award in the British honours system after the Victoria Cross, recognising "acts of the greatest heroism or for most conspicuous courage in circumstance of extreme danger". In death he became the only Australian serviceman to be awarded both the George Cross and the Military Cross and the most highly decorated individual in the history of the Australian Signals Corps.

Chapter 7

C FORCE

The accommodation was not first class.
The accommodation was not economy class.
It wasn't 100th class – it was absolutely zilch class.
The ship was also carrying hundreds of Japanese troops
and civilians, so our lot was bunked down in the only
space that remained, on the open deck,
a mere 2000 of us!

Private Jack Chapman, 8th Division Signals[1]

In late 1942 the Japanese stepped up their program of sending large contingents of prisoners of war from Singapore to work as slave labour across the Greater East Asia Co-Prosperity Sphere, the Orwellian euphemism for the lands subjugated by Japanese imperialism. The most infamous destinations were the Thai–Burma railway and Sandakan in Borneo, but prisoners were also sent to work in Manchuria, Indo-China, Formosa, Korea and Japan itself.

Doug Lush and his men were part of the group designated as 'C Force' and they were headed for Japan. The 563 Australians were under the leadership of Lieutenant Colonel Andrew Robertson, who had been commanding officer of the 2/20 Battalion. They were drawn mainly from among those prisoners who had so far been held at the Adam Park, Havelock Road and Sime Road satellite camps. They included large numbers of men from the 2/18th, 2/19th, 2/20th and 2/30th battalions as well as the 8th Division Signals. The men would be split into two groups in Japan. About 250 led by Captain John Paterson and including Lieutenants Doug Lush and Ken Trumble were destined for the city of Kobe and a camp officially known as Osaka Number 5-D. The rest were to travel with Colonel Robertson to Naoetsu on the north-west coast of the main island of Honshu – Tokyo Number 4 Branch Camp.

At around 3pm on 28 November 1942, the men of C Force were taken to Singapore harbour and transferred by small motor launches to their transport, the *Kamakura Maru*. Built in Scotland and launched in 1929, the 15,000-ton vessel had been a luxury passenger ship plying the northern Pacific between Yokohama and San Francisco in the decade before the war. None of the comforts for which the ship was well known would extend to the wretched men who were the last to board before embarkation from Singapore. In addition to the Australians, there were about 950 Dutch POWs, 500 American servicemen and a small number of Royal Air Force personnel. The prisoners also included a number of senior officers, among them Lieutenant General Lewis Heath, who had commanded the British III Indian Corps, and Brigadier Duncan Maxwell, commander of the Australian 27th Brigade.

The *Kamakura Maru* also carried a strange additional cargo. Four white boxes had been placed reverently in one of the upper deck cabins on a large altar in front of a Rising Sun flag. They contained the ashes of four Japanese submariners who died in the audacious midget submarine attack on Sydney Harbour on 31 May 1942. The ashes had already travelled far. In August, Japanese ambassador Kuwai Tatsuo and a party of embassy officials and their families had carried the boxes with their luggage when they were repatriated from Melbourne to the neutral port of Laurenco Marques in Portuguese East Africa. From there, they were brought to Singapore.

The morning after the *Kamakura Maru* departed Singapore, the ship stopped off the south-east tip of the Malayan peninsula to take aboard a group of nine Japanese women with an escort of armed marines. Doug Lush and other Australian prisoners speculated that the women may have been the wives or other relatives of the dead submariners who had been brought to accompany the ashes of their loved ones on the final leg of their journey home to a heroes' welcome.

The cabins that had been set aside to place the ashes became something of a sacred site on the ship, Lush recalled: "Any prisoners needing to pass the cabins were required to bow low and purposefully in honour of these sailors' memory or else any one of the guards whose task it was to protect those remains would quickly reprimand the unfortunate Australian, or other such POWs, by the use of a rifle butt or anything else which was handy to strike them."

The Australian Government's decision to assist the repatriation of the ashes, after the bodies of the submariners had been cremated with full ceremonial honours, was applauded by the Japanese authorities. Radio Tokyo described it as a chivalrous act by Australia that "greatly impresses" Japan. But there would be no sign of chivalry in the treatment of the Australian prisoners aboard the *Kamakura Maru* during the week-long voyage to Nagasaki. While the Dutch and American prisoners were held in cramped and stifling conditions in the lower decks among the cargo, the Australians were exposed in equally crowded circumstances aft of the first and second-class decks.

Signaller Lloyd Ellerman recorded the ordeal in his diary: "We suffered days of extreme discomfort, open to the elements and the ship's wash and with little to eat – two meals a day of four ounces of rice! We sat back to back, had no room to lie down and could sleep only fitfully. There were no washing facilities for us while sanitary arrangements were abominable. A primitive, temporary and very open 'loo' was perched on the edge of the ship proper, with an overhang over the side of the ship."[2]

The meagre rice ration was of poor quality and riddled with weevils. Sickness soon spread among the prisoners, especially those held below deck. The *benjos* (toilets) were large poles suspended from the ship's stern, hanging out hazardously over the rails with the sea below. Prisoners heeding nature's call would have to hold on grimly to either side, and hope they wouldn't slip or be washed overboard. In that event, the prisoners all knew they would be left to drown.

As grim as the *benjos* were, those held above deck at least had access without the steep climb up narrow stairways experienced by those sweltering below. For those Dutch, American and British POWs below, where dysentery was rife, this would soon become an even greater cause for more sickness to spread among those prisoners battened down in the ship's hold. Down in these darkened quarters, many would not even make it to these stairways, as they navigated their way through the maze of their comrades before their bodies betrayed them. The Australian officers were held in a passageway leading to the first-class lounge. Conditions there were even more cramped than those experienced by the rest of the men on the two upper decks. Sleep was almost impossible.

Two days out from Singapore, the ship was making about 14 knots and was already well into the South China Sea in generally calm weather, following a zigzagging course to avoid contact with any enemy ships or aircraft. As they nursed their discomfort and brooded on what horrors and deprivations might lay ahead of them, the thoughts of many of the men turned to the possibility of escape. Many of the 2000 Allied prisoners aboard the *Kamakura Maru* were well aware that they greatly outnumbered the Japanese and could well take control of the ship. The Japanese were only lightly armed with a single captured Bren machine-gun mounted overlooking the rear of the decks.

According to Doug Lush, the most popular scenario mulled over in furtive conversations among the prisoners was to sail the captured ship to a Russian port. Others argued that it would be possible to reach the United States territories in Micronesia. But such ideas were soon dispelled by wiser heads. One of the senior Dutch naval officers on board argued that any attempt to take over the ship would be pure folly. He pointed out that the ship was almost certainly being tracked by Japanese submarines or other vessels and under regular radio monitoring from Japan. Every merchant ship had its own security code, and these were changed on a periodic basis by the Japanese admiralty. Each ship was required to call in via radio at a specific time in order for the naval authorities to be able to plot their progress. Should the *Kamakura Maru* fail to call in as required and with the correct call sign, a search would soon follow, and, as she was sailing between Japanese occupied territories, aircraft could quickly be scrambled in response. As Doug Lush lamented: "With these realities, our dreams of a quick exit were exactly that, dreams."

On 3 December excitement stirred among the prisoners when three Japanese ships, sailing in close formation, came into view. They were evidently bound for Manila from Japan. Cooler breezes began to sweep over the ship's decks, reminding the Australians, after many months in the tropics, that they were without winter-issue clothes – a fact that would soon be an additional cause of suffering.

The next day, 4 December, the *Kamakura Maru* reached Tainan, on the south-west tip of the island of Formosa (Taiwan). The officers had recently been advised that this was where General Heath, Brigadier Maxwell and others of the rank of major and above, apart from Colonel Robertson, would be disembarking. Many of the most senior Allied officers were held on Formosa before being transferred to Manchuria and Korea later in the war. After stopping for a few hours while the officers were transferred to the shore aboard motor launches, the ship resumed its passage to Japan. Now the weather began to turn sharply cooler and the seas changed from calm to rough. For many of the prisoners, the sufferings of hunger and illness were now joined by seasickness. Captain John Paterson noted that the Dutch prisoners, some 60 per cent of whom were 'coloured' troops, seemed to fare worst of all from the harsher conditions: "Some of the men are seasick and the decks are one hell of a mess. The Dutchmen seem to be feeling the cold, and are huddled together like a lot of animals."[3]

As the *Kamakura Maru* began to move through the southernmost islands of Japan, the weather eased. By mid-morning on 5 December there was a fresh wave of excitement aboard the ship as a Japanese dive-bomber suddenly swooped down over the ship and then proceeded to circle it. The prisoners concluded this was a prearranged meeting for security reasons and, after the pilot was satisfied all was in order, the plane disappeared back into the clouds and was not seen again. Soon after, the Australian officers were finally made aware of their destination. This was to be Nagasaki, a major port located on the island of Kyushu, and the ship was due to dock there the following day.

The prisoners finally reached Nagasaki on 7 December 1942. During the voyage from Singapore, 10 of them had perished and all had suffered from the appalling conditions in which they were held on board. But they were also lucky to have made it to Japan without being attacked by Allied vessels. Late the following April the *Kamakura Maru* departed Manila for Balikpapan carrying a cargo of heavy military vehicles and ammunition and 2500 passengers including Japanese naval personnel, oil production workers and 150 women. As she crossed the Sulu Sea unescorted but zigzagging to avoid detection, the ship was intercepted by the USS *Gudgeon*, a Tambour-class submarine. The *Gudgeon*'s captain, Lieutenant Commander William S. Post, ordered a spread of four torpedoes to be fired from a range of 3200 yards – two of them hitting the *Kamakura Maru* starboard side in her no. 4 hold and auxiliary machinery compartment, triggering a severe fire in the vessel's stern. Within 12 minutes she upended from the stern and sank. Only 28 of the 176 naval crew and 437 passengers would survive.

On their arrival in Nagasaki, the Australians were required to remain aboard for yet another night. During the interlude, Captain Paterson had time to describe, in his hidden diary, the scene that greeted their arrival:

> We reached the first port of Japan at 1000 hours and stopped for about ½ an hour then moved past several islands before we got to this port. To reach it, we came through magnificent harbours like fiords; close to the shore with cliffs towering above the ship. We passed an island practically covered with modern buildings, and it looks like a naval establishment. On one side of the fiord we are now in, the cliffs are studded with hovels – hundreds of them; on the other side is a shipbuilding yard with a few vessels on the stocks. On both sides there are a few oil tanks. The whole place appears to be like a Norwegian fishing village, although a bit bigger. It is now 1600 hours, and the Yanks and British troops are disembarking. We don't go off until tomorrow morning when we are to leave by train for Kobe, 300 miles further north. It is bitterly cold, and we are very hungry. We still get only a plate of rice twice a day, with a cup of tea.[4]

While they waited to disembark, the Australian officers were further briefed on the Japanese plans to split the prisoners into two groups, with Colonel Robertson accompanying the larger group of about 300 men to Naoetsu, and the remainder, under the command of Captain Paterson, bound for Kobe. In addition to Doug Lush, the other officers assigned to Paterson's group were lieutenants Ken Stevens, Reg Hastings, Reg Crane and Ken Trumble, all of the 8th Division Signals. In addition, they were joined by Captain William Bathgate and Lieutenant Ralph Johnson from the 22nd Infantry Brigade headquarters staff, Captain Frank Beverley from the 2/19th Battalion and the 2/30th Battalion's Lieutenant Charles Furner. Along with the Australians was a group of about 150 Dutch personnel, bringing the Kobe party to about 400 men.

The task of leading these men into what was certain to be an arduous and indefinite ordeal in the land of their Japanese conquerors weighed heavily on John Paterson as he prepared to go ashore: "I feel that it is a big responsibility, as I now have supreme control and the job of seeing to the welfare of all these men with goodness knows what sort of trouble ahead of us."[5]

Chapter 8

KOBE

Much has been written about the treatment of various
groups of POWs. The treatment of the Kobe men,
while somewhat different, had a common thread of
bestiality, bashings and starvation.

Private Lloyd Ellerman, 8th Division Signals[1]

The morning after their arrival in Nagasaki, the Australians and
the Dutch troops still being held below deck were at last allowed to
disembark. A ferry was brought alongside to transfer the men from
the anchorage in the harbour to the shore. Finally back on dry land,
the prisoners were ordered to assemble on the wharf for a head count
by the Japanese guards. As had been the case back in Singapore, the
process seemed interminable as the guards counted and recounted
those present, to the rising irritation of the men.

The prisoners were kept on the wharf for about five hours – without
food and in freezing conditions – before they were separated into two
parties and marched under close escort to the city's modern central
railway station. Here they were again counted before boarding sep-
arate trains. At about 9pm they were issued with their first meal of
the day – a small box containing three rice cakes, three small pieces
of fish and some daikon, a type of radish. The food was strange but
enjoyable. "Excellent feed," Ken Trumble noted in his diary. Little did

the diners know that it would be their last satisfying meal for the next couple of years.

Colonel Robertson and his men had been the first to be herded into the awaiting carriages, which they found, to their delight, were heated – a welcome respite from the biting cold they had been forced to ensure throughout the long day. This would be the last time the two groups of C Force men would see each other – at least for the duration of the war and, in so many cases, ever.

Robertson's group departed on what was to be a 750-mile journey over two full days north to the small industrial city of Naoetsu, 200 miles north-west of Tokyo. Here they would become labourers in a stainless-steel plant and adjacent chemical works. Their camp – known as the No. 4 Tokyo Branch Camp – was initially housed in a salt warehouse of the Shin-etsu Chemical Company. Naoetsu would soon earn its reputation as the most infamous of the prison camps scattered across Japan, a place of unrelenting hardship and brutality. At the end of the war, 15 of the Naoetsu guards would be tried for war crimes and eight of them would be executed. Of the 300 men who boarded the train in Nagasaki with Robertson on 9 December 1942, 60 would perish.

Among those to succumb to pneumonia, malnutrition and exhaustion during that first, bitter winter was Andrew Robertson himself, as Australia's official history of the war recorded: "Robertson, weakened by starvation and sickness, died of meningitis in March 1943, having been forced to run four miles every morning for the two months preceding his death. The wearing of overcoats was forbidden within barracks buildings although the temperature even within walls fell below zero during the winter months and snow drifts were as deep as 16 feet."[2]

The most notorious of the Naoetsu guards was Sergeant Mutsuhiro Watanabe, known as The Birdman, who ruthlessly beat and tortured many of the prisoners under his charge. At the end of the war, General Douglas MacArthur listed Watanabe at 23 among the 40 most sought after war criminals, but the French-speaking guard managed to evade capture for several years and charges against him were eventually dropped. Among the prisoners held at Naoetsu who suffered at the hands of Watanabe was the American airman Louis Zamperini. A celebrated middle-distance runner who competed at the 1936 Berlin Olympics, Zamperini had survived 47 days drifting in the Pacific Ocean after his bomber crashed into the sea – only to face the further ordeals of captivity. Zamperini's remarkable story of endurance and survival would be told in an autobiography that became the 2014 movie *Unbroken*, directed by Angelina Jolie.

The Australian prisoners had arrived in Japan at the beginning of the northern winter. In the months that followed, the country was to endure its coldest season in 70 years. For the troops of the 8th Division, who had had been serving in the tropics for between 12 and 18 months and most of whom had come with only summer clothing, it was a shocking transition that would compound their suffering.

After the train carrying Robertson and his men left Nagasaki for Naoetsu, the remaining 250 Australians under Captain John Paterson and the 150 Dutch prisoners aboard the second train prepared to depart for Kobe, where they would be put to work at the Kawasaki shipyard. A debate soon developed between the Australians and the Dutch as to who was the senior officer and therefore should take charge of the group. While the most senior Dutchman was a naval Lieutenant Commander, Ben Welvaadt – whose rank had equivalent seniority to an army major – the Dutch agreed to recognise Paterson's leadership.

The train for Kobe left just before midnight with an escort of four Japanese army NCOs and a dozen guards. The prisoners were ordered to keep the carriage blinds drawn so that they could not be seen, but at daylight they were able to get some of their first views of rural Japan glimpsed through slits in the blinds. They were passing through hilly country close to the coast and a series of big industrial plants. Light snowfalls punctuated their journey. At a series of stops, they were well fed – compared with what was soon to come – with cardboard lunchboxes containing fish, pickles and vegetables. Around midday an electric tractor was coupled to the train to haul it through the four-mile-long tunnel connecting the islands of Kyushu and Honshu. They reached Kobe a few minutes after midnight – 10 December 1942 – concluding their 24-hour odyssey.

After alighting from the train, the prisoners were again lined up to be counted to make sure none had absconded during the journey from Nagasaki. Once satisfied that all prisoners were present and accounted for, the men were ordered to march out under escort to their new prison home in the suburb of Takatori Michi, nestled in the hills about four miles from the centre of Kobe.

The newly constructed camp was built on the two-acre site of a children's playground. There were three large barracks huts built of pine and split bamboo, two lavatory rooms, a recreational hall, a kitchen, an administration block and a boiler room containing a huge 3000 gallon bath. Each of the barracks huts was about 20 feet wide and 120 feet long with rows of double bunks and floors covered with straw matting. The huts were also fitted with loudspeakers from which orders would be delivered from the administration block.

On their arrival, the men were marched onto the camp parade ground where they were addressed by the newly appointed commandant,

Lieutenant Yasuji Morimoto. A slightly built, 37-year-old former farmer, Morimoto struggled to capture the air of military authority he craved. He would soon be nicknamed 'Bonnie Leslie' after the pig in the popular Australian radio serial *Dad and Dave*. That would be contracted to the safer shorthand of 'BL' or 'Leslie' in various secret diaries kept at great risk by some of the men over the months ahead.

Morimoto had accompanied the men on the train journey from Nagasaki, occupying the officers' compartment. Having discarded his riding boots he had "slept for the most part of the journey, with two or three toes protruding through his white socks".[3] After waking, he had led a gruelling interrogation of Captain Paterson and the other officers. The postwar official history of the Signals Corps would cast Morimoto as "an utter scoundrel in his dealings with the POWs".

Harold Stephen Kildey was a Lance Corporal with the 2/10 Field Ambulance. Born and raised on a small farm near Griffith in the New South Wales Riverina district, 'Mick' Kildey was still a teenager when he had enlisted in 1941. His first encounter with the man who would rule his life and the lives of his 250 fellow Australians over the many months ahead was at the first camp parade:

> There was this little runt of a Jap. He hopped onto the platform with his jackboots and big sword hanging at his side. His name was Morimoto and as soon as we were standing at attention he shouted out three words. I'm not sure what they meant but it sounded like 'Anonair – Immuggera – Kurrywah'. I think it may have meant 'Pay attention you bloody fools', or something like that. He shouted out another word and the guards that were surrounding us all jammed a round up the spout and I thought to myself 'Gee, this doesn't look too good'.[4]

As the guards trained their weapons on the prisoners, Morimoto read from a prepared statement that was then translated into English.

To: All Prisoners of War

From: Commander of Osaka POW Camp

Recently most prisoners of war are working very conscientiously but there are still some whose attitude is not what it should be. It seems to me you are forgetting just where you are standing. You fought to protect your colours, for which I honour you as soldiers, but at the same time our people will not forget that you shot at our brothers and sons, killed some of them and wounded others. To this fact you must pay your toll very heavily. You fought well but lost and were taken captives. It would be all natural and possible that you would be standing before a firing squad before long. However, by the august virtues and grace of His Majesty, The Emperor, and also benevolence of our military authorities, you are still sound and alive, having necessary quarters to live in with clothing and food properly supplied. Moreover, you are allowed to communicate with your loved ones. Did this fact ever occur in your mind? If not, just stop and think it over. If there are any who do not live up to our expectations in every respect, those are the ones who forget about the fact. We are doing our utmost to make your life comfortable under the circumstances. Our treatment is fair and impartial in regard with our military laws as well as the International Treaties. This fact should be appreciated, although we are not insisting it. When you work hard, you may think that you are helping your enemy, and by slacking down on your work or disobeying our orders you may think you are doing your country justice. It may be true, but it is certainly not doing justice to yourselves, because we are watching over all POW individually and keeping daily records in every respect so that when the time comes for your return to your country we will give the first preference to the best ones and those who dare not do their best will probably never get the chance to join their loved ones. So it is only natural that you should do your tasks conscientiously to acquire your freedom and join your beloved ones at the earliest date. To conclude this statement, I shall like to say that to acquire freedom there is always hardships and sacrifices. Without the hardships and sacrifices freedom can never be acquired. Bear this in mind, never to forget, and then you would know how you should behave in the future.

The extent of "the emperor's grace" was evident as soon as Morimoto left the parade ground. Despite their long journey, the late hour and the cold conditions, one of the guards declared there would be no rest until all of the 400 assembled prisoners had learned to count in Japanese, as Doug Lush recalled: "The Japanese said nobody was to leave the parade until they could count to one hundred. It was bloody cold but we just had to stand there and they tested us over and over. We all had to all number off, 'Ichi, Ni, San, etc'. It took about two or three hours to do this, before we were dismissed." As the drilling continued, the guards would walk along the rows of assembled prisoners with wooden swords and would hit the prisoners over the head or the shoulders for any slight mistakes.

When the ordeal was finally over, the men were escorted to the huts. Inside each hut were two rows of double bunks. Across the concrete floors were a series of small holes where charcoal fires could be lit. It was very cramped. Each prisoner was allocated a two by one yard tatami mat to sleep on and five blankets. There was enthusiasm about the blankets until it was realised that they were made out of wood fibre. "When you got into them they went around you like a tree trunk," Lush remembered. "We had to pummel them up to make them fit over our bodies, but they were blankets, and essential in that winter."

Early the next morning the men were again called out on parade with all of their gear. All knives, scissors, tools, blade razors, cards, chess and draughts sets, cigarette lighters and matches were confiscated – plus more that the guards chose to souvenir. "Japs took pretty well anything they fancied for themselves. BBs [bloody bastards]!" Ken Trumble lamented in his diary.[5] Each of the men was then issued with a uniform – green dyed hessian pants and a green hessian jacket with a red and white stripe across the shoulders at the back. On the front of each jacket was a number that had been sewn on. Lush was number six. Trumble was eight. "Finally, they gave each of us a red Japanese cap," Lush recalled. "And that was our uniform to work in and to live in and it didn't last very long at all. Fortunately when the ship was leaving Singapore, we had been issued with British uniforms out of storage. The Japanese had taken them from us but later gave them back to us to wear, which was a saving grace as the Japanese uniforms lasted practically no time at all."

After being issued with the uniforms, the men were given factory numbers as well as their prison camp numbers, as Lloyd Ellerman recalled: "We were harangued by various Nip officers and told quite plainly that we worked or we didn't get fed – rather a short argument. We had photos taken and we were weighed. The latter was a curious exercise because they didn't again show any concern for our body weight – which fell dramatically throughout the whole period of imprisonment."[6]

All of the men were then interrogated about their past and what they had been doing in private life before the war. The questioning appeared designed to establish what work they might be given at the shipyard. Lush and the other officers urged the men to confuse the process by saying they had all been farmers. They were all then required to complete a bizarre "impressions questionnaire". According to Lush, the questions were:

1. What is your favourite occupation?

2. What are your thoughts whilst at work?

3. What did you expect of Nippon? What is your impression since you have arrived?

4. What is your opinion of present war situation?

5. What is your impression of Xmas spent in Nippon?

6. What are your impressions with regard to the funeral for your comrades?

The men were then instructed that they would now be working for the Japanese Emperor at the Kawasaki shipyard and the work would be to support the Japanese economy, not the war effort, which impressed none of the new workforce, according to Lush: "A lot of the Australians said, 'Be buggered, we don't want to bloody work for the Japanese war effort'. Well, a couple of days later it was all resolved because the Japs turned around and said, 'OK. No work, no eat!' That was the start of two and half years of bloody hard work. These men would be worked fifteen hours straight, with only two rest days a month."

Rollcall became a daily ritual at the camp. Each of the huts had a designated prisoner in charge. As leader of the camp, Captain Paterson would oversee the rollcall assisted by the other officers, including Doug Lush and Ken Trumble, before presenting a report to the guards. Paterson remained on duty throughout their time at the Kobe camp, apart from a period of about four months when he was bedridden with dysentery. While ill, he was cared for by his batman, Lance Sergeant Ken Cowell, a signaller from New South Wales. Cowell had been a tailor in civilian life and would mend the threadbare shirts and other clothes for some of the men. His devotion to Paterson during this time almost certainly saved the officer's life.

Another daily ritual was the meal parade. Buckets of rice were distributed between groups of 20 men and rice had to be prepared for those who were going out through the day for work. The men would then assemble at 7am each morning on the parade ground. The Kawasaki officials and guards would take over from the camp guards and move the men out to go to the shipyard.

While the officers were in charge, day-to-day responsibility for managing the men in the camp and at the shipyard – including a large contingent of British prisoners who had arrived before the Australians and the Dutch – fell to the non-commissioned officers (NCOs). The British group included four warrant officers but the most senior Australian NCO was Des Mulcahy, who held the more junior rank of sergeant. On the first night at Kobe, Mulcahy was called to an urgent meeting with the officers and told that, while the Australian prisoners wouldn't work under 'the Pommies', the British prisoners might accept an Australian NCO as leader. He was immediately promoted: "That's how I came to be made a warrant officer but I never got paid for it. I only ever got paid sergeant fees the whole time, although I was doing a colonel's job really … When it came to the work party, everything fell on me, so I was responsible to take the work party out and bring the work party home. Any trouble with the work party, it was my problem."[7]

The POW officers, who were not required to work, would remain behind in camp with the prisoners who were sick and the kitchen staff. They were responsible for maintaining the camp, supervising daily cleaning by those troops who were not at the shipyard, organising the rice rations and negotiating with the Japanese for any coal that was needed.

The Japanese knew the Australians had built the roadway around the shrine back in Singapore and the men believed they had been selected to go to Japan because they were regarded as good workers. It seemed at the outset that they would be relatively well treated to ensure they were able to work hard. That illusion was soon shattered.

Chapter 9

KAWASAKI

And so the first long day turned into the first long
week, the first long month and then year.

Private Jack Chapman, 8th Division Signals[1]

In 1878 Japanese industrialist Shinzo Kawasaki founded a shipbuilding company that would immortalise his family name as a global brand and create one of the pillars of the modern Japanese economy. Eight years after opening their first shipyard in Tokyo, Kawasaki and his partner, Vice Finance Minister Matsukata Masayoshi, opened a second dockyard on a promontory on the south-western edge of the harbour at Kobe. By the outbreak of World War I, the Kawasaki Dockyard Company had grown into an engineering behemoth that manufactured battleships, aircraft carriers and submarines for the Japanese military as well as commercial vessels, locomotives, automobiles and aircraft. By World War II, Kawasaki was an indispensable cog in the Japanese military machine and its militarist ambitions.

The Kawasaki company had also played an important role in forging ties between the Japanese and German militaries between the wars. In 1921 the Japanese Navy sent Matsukata Kojiro, the founder's son and then president of the company, on a tour of Europe during which he was deeply impressed by the advances in German shipbuilding.

He invited a team of German engineers to Japan and Kawasaki subsequently began constructing submarines based on German models.[2] Swastika-flagged vessels and their crews would become a common sight for the Australian prisoners in Kobe as the war dragged on.

Two weeks after their arrival at Kobe, most of the men were sent off from the camp to work at the vast Kawasaki shipyard. It was about a three-quarter mile walk from the camp to the Takatori Michi railway station from where the men would be taken by train to the main station at Kobe. From there, it was another two-mile march to the shipyard.

Many of the men were to be employed on large machines, cutting, drilling and bending plates of steel which were fitted on the hulls of aircraft carriers, tankers and merchant ships. Some were assigned to work alongside Japanese workers as 'dogmen' loading up the steel sections, while others would be placed into riveting gangs where they would work on various parts of the shipbuilding. Soon there would be nicknames for most of the guards at the shipyard and the camp, none of them complimentary – Sleepy, Kewpie, Smiler, Boof, Sweet Alice, The Professor. Thousands of Japanese civilians were also employed at the shipyard, some of them teenagers. Most seemed intent on doing as little as they could get away with, as Lloyd Ellerman observed: "We POWs were happy to adopt the same attitude. Everyone did as little work as possible. In our case – riveting on ships – we learned how to drive rivets into steel plates, making them faulty, but in some cases not discovered, and done again. It gave us quite a kick to do these pranks. In other words, we never yielded to the will of our captors."[3]

Much of the work was extremely dangerous and there would be many casualties. At lot of the equipment had been built in England before World War I and was in poor condition. Some of the cranes didn't work properly, so if a big sheet of metal had to be moved, the Japanese would line up 10 or 12 prisoners who would be forced to carry the sheet on their shoulders. "You had a permanent gang there some days," Des Mulcahy recalled. "They would be all day carrying these big steel sheets of metal. If one man dropped it, the whole lot had to get away otherwise they would all get crushed. It was very primitive."[4]

The prisoners became expert at forcing delays to their work. Fires would go out. Rivets would run out. Necessary scaffolding would go missing. Alex Dandie, a POW who served with the 2/30th Battalion, published in the early 1990s a history of J Force – the party of 300 Australians who sailed from Singapore on 16 May 1943, including some who were sent to the Kobe area. "Whenever we did any stevedoring on ships in Kobe Harbour, we saw an aircraft carrier beached outside the artificial wall of the harbour," Dandie wrote. "When launched, it immediately began to take on water because the POWs working on the riveting of the plates, so it was said, were able to leave a rivet every so often so badly fixed that it did not hold when the launching took place."[5]

Beside the shipyard's dry dock were pens for Japanese midget submarines. Mick Kildey recalled regularly seeing seven or eight of them there when they were brought in to be provisioned and refuelled: "We never saw them being loaded or anything like that but they were there all the time and I can tell you they were a nasty looking piece of work."[6]

There were also regular visits to the shipyard by German vessels through the course of 1943 – sometimes accompanied by furtive acts of kindness from one Caucasian adversary to another. Large German submarines would dock about 200 yards from where the men were working. "The German sailors used to come ashore to wash at the tanks along the wharf," said Kildey. "The blokes somehow or other used to sneak down and there would be some cigarettes or soap left on the tank stand. So really they could see the hardships we were under and they were doing their little bit to make life easier for some of our fellows."[7]

Soon after they began work at the shipyard, the prisoners were given a bizarre order by the Kobe camp commandant, Lieutenant Morimoto, to give their written impressions about the qualities of the Japanese Navy, as Jack Chapman recalled: "Our replies were, of course, very much to the point. We told Morimoto just what he wanted to hear. Nothing dull or strange about us. The Jap Navy had great ships, great sailors and officers. Great navy!"[8]

One prisoner, however, decided to say what he really thought. Jack Crockett, a private with the 2/19th Battalion, was a 40-year old accountant who had worked on the New Guinea goldfields before the war. Educated, intelligent and somewhat disdainful of his younger fellow prisoners, Crockett was inclined to speak – and write – his mind. "Our friend Jack told Morimoto what he thought, actually what we all thought but were too smart to say to their faces," Kildey recalled. "All Japanese ships were copies of Western naval ships, Jack wrote. Japan as a naval power was a no-no. Their sailors were coolie class, officers no better, poorly trained, typical 'Made in Japan' stuff. Did I say Jack was intelligent? After Morimoto digested the written and signed replies, Jack was singled out, escorted to the admin building, beaten severely and, together with other damaged parts, had his jaw broken. He was of course refused medical treatment and it was weeks before he could eat properly."[9]

The work at the shipyard was arduous, especially when the weather was extreme, and often dangerous, according to Lloyd Ellerman: "We had some nasty accidents. We worked on large tankers which stretched forty feet to the deck when the holds were fully built. In the winter months, the cold was awful as we were perched so far up and often at the stern, over the bay. The wind and the sleet were hard to take. We were so thin that the wind went straight through us."[10]

Accidents were a regular occurrence, some of them fatal. An English prisoner suffered a broken leg. Another's hand was crushed. In both cases, gangrene set in. The only treatment available was to sear the wounds with a red-hot poker from the camp cookhouse. And there were many narrow escapes.

Bondi-born Jack Chapman and his elder brother Bob had enlisted together at the Sydney Showgrounds at Moore Park on the same day, 15 April 1941, and received consecutive service numbers: NX72914 and NX72915. Their brother Colin joined the infantry and fought in New Guinea, as Bob recalled: "They issued little badges to the mothers and on the badge was a star to show you had a son or daughter in the war. My mother wore one with three stars. She was very proud."[11]

Jack and Bob had fought and been captured together in Singapore and were now imprisoned together at Kobe. They would credit each other with their survival through three and a half years internment and eventual return home. One day at the shipyard in 1943 would be proof enough of the importance of looking out for each other, as Bob recounted: "Our job was fitting steel sheets to the side of the boat frame using big bolts and big spanners. If you stripped a bolt it was easy to lose your balance … One time I was working high up on the side of the boat and Jack slipped. I reckon he was on his way down and would have gone if I hadn't grabbed him and held him. If I hadn't been there that day he would never have made it. There was no protection from falling if you overbalanced or did something silly."[12]

Lloyd Ellerman credits the Australian creed of mateship with making the difference between life and death for himself and many of his fellow prisoners: "Each prisoner has to thank his comrades for his survival. The spirit was the same in every camp – a silent bonding together of men in a tough situation, needing one another to survive. The mateship was silent and automatic. We were living like animals working under appalling conditions, yet there was humour about, and a pride in being Australian, and feeling superior to our captors."[13]

In May 1943, Signalman Bob Flanagan became the first of the Australian POWs to be killed in an accident at the shipyard. Flanagan, a 31-year-old lance corporal from Queensland, fell to his death while working high up on the hull of one of the ships under construction. He would leave behind a wife and young daughter in the small town of Mitchell on Queensland's Darling Downs.

During the preceding five months, 17 other Kobe prisoners had died of illness, unmourned by their captors. But the first fatal accident at the shipyard appeared to shock the Japanese. As Flanagan had died on the job, they decided he should receive a formal funeral, as John Paterson recorded in his diary: "A marquee tent was erected on the parade ground and at the back of it on both sides was draped a black and white canvas. The coffin was brought out and placed in the tent. The men returned from work at 1300 hours and paraded at 1500, the Australians wearing their Aussie hats and looking very spruce."[14]

After a prayer and the reading of the 23rd Psalm, there were addresses by Paterson and Lieutenant Morimoto, the camp commandant, who paid tribute to Flanagan's supposed sacrifice for the Emperor before declaring that in future the prisoners had to be more careful at the shipyard. Flowers were placed on the coffin by Morimoto, an official from the shipyard and Flanagan's comrades, Paterson recorded: "After that, the pallbearers carried the coffin to a waiting hearse which I accompanied with the medical sergeant to the crematorium, about three miles away ... Coming home, the Chev car in which we were riding (on charcoal) broke down, so we had to walk the rest of the way. Altogether there were 14 civilians from the shipyards, 12 Army representatives, 3 photographers, present at the service, which some thought very impressive."

If the event suggested that the Japanese were about to extend a humanitarian hand to their sick and hungry slaves, it was a cruel illusion.

Chapter 10

SICKNESS

Another death – an Australian, Private George Dunne
– from pneumonia. This is a terrible shock.
Makes me wonder what will happen next. The needless
waste of young life is appalling, and our inability
to do anything for these men is terrible.

Diary of Captain John Paterson, 15 March 1943

In March 1943 representatives of the International Red Cross visited the Kobe camp for the first time. The Japanese went to great lengths to pretend that conditions for their prisoners were far better and far more humane than the grim truth of endemic sickness, desperate hunger and unrelenting physical abuse.

Just before the arrival of the Red Cross team, the Japanese placed a sign on one of the administrative huts saying 'Canteen'. The camp did not have a canteen but in the window of the hut with the freshly erected sign were placed a variety of foods and other items, none of which the prisoners were allowed near and all of which were removed as soon as the perfunctory visit was over. Shipments of Red Cross parcels were regularly sent to POWs in the camps in Japan throughout the war but during the two and a half years that the Australians were at Kobe they received only six parcels each.

Most of the 51 deaths of Allied prisoners at the Kobe camp –
including the 18 Australians who perished – were caused by the lethal
combination of malnutrition and pneumonia. When prisoners fell ill,
their mates would rally to nurse them through the period of danger
as best they could, as Jack Chapman remembered:

> Pneumonia was the biggest danger. When this rotten illness put
> one of us into the hospital, he was fed with the best from our
> meagre supplies until he became stronger, or if fate was to be
> unkind, until he died. We all got to know the symptoms and the
> subsequent routine: a fever, a deterioration for a week or two, the
> inescapable climax which every patient dreaded and then either
> slow recovery or death. Our mate Jimmy O'Connell went down
> with it and each afternoon after returning from the shipyards
> the small group of us, Bob, Jim Whitley, Hammer, Tod Morgan
> and myself would go straight to the hospital and sit with the sick
> one, telling him whopper lies, anything to cheer him up, home
> by whenever and all the food we would pig out on.[1]

The attitude of the guards often made the situation worse for the men
who were ill, as Doug Lush recalled: "When I was taking the camp
through physical exercises the Japs would have all the sick men brought
out. They would have to take off their shirts and it was bloody cold
weather too. They would have these scrubbing brushes and we'd have
to scrub all over. The Japs would say that it was good for our health."

After enduring a long and bitter winter, the northern spring of 1943
brought no relief, as Lloyd Ellerman remembered:

> The advent of spring reminded us of home but it brought much
> trouble in the shape of pneumonia and bronchial pneumonia, apart
> from the more chronic dysentery/diarrhoea, beri beri etc. The men
> went down like flies and the hospital couldn't handle the really
> sick. I recall 187 men sick out of the then four hundred POWs.

All this didn't please the Japanese one bit and they showed their worst side over it. They would force ill men to set off for work and some collapsed soon after marching out of the gates. Only then would they be accepted as ill. It was also quite normal for an average of 10 men per day to collapse at the shipyards. Our medical orderlies rendered all possible care and attention – in fact they were marvellous – but losses from pneumonia were suffered. The orderlies just had to watch their patients and hope the heart would last through the crisis period.[2]

The Kobe camp did not have a medical officer. The original C Force medical officer had been sent with Colonel Robertson's group to Naoetsu. The Japanese assigned two of their soldiers as medical orderlies, known among the men as Dopey and Sleepy. One of the Dutch prisoners, Lieutenant Konrad Eyckman, declared himself to have had some medical training. In fact, in civilian life he had been a veterinarian. Eyckman ran the camp 'hospital' with the help of two medical orderlies originally from the 2/10th Field Ambulance. One of them was Corporal George Blues, a 23-year-old former steam locomotive driver from Townsville.

There were no anaesthetics in the camp, so operations would be performed with Corporal Blues holding the patient in a headlock. One English POW had a growth on his skull. The Japanese would not help, so the man, in great pain, asked Eyckman to intervene. The Dutchman made an incision and drained off the fluid, which was about half a cup full. This eased the pressure and the man was back at work within a month.

Len Curry of the 2/19th Battalion had a cancerous growth on his lip. The doctor at Changi had said that he would need 'ray treatment' on his return to Australia. The growth spread, so Curry asked Eyckman if he would attempt to remove it. On one *yasumi* (rest) day, the Dutchman heated irons in the cookhouse fire. Len's head was held down and the growth burnt. The crude treatment took two days to complete but was successful.[3]

Eyckman was also called on to serve as the camp dentist. According to Signalman Jack Bromley, one of his first patients was a prisoner named Cliff Portia: "Portia had a tooth removed, but it was the wrong one. The Dutchman said not to worry, then removed the correct one. I remember his dedication to helping the POWs and his help, humour, and friendship to me. He mended my hand, leg, etcetera and cured my pneumonia and dysentery."[4]

Many of Eyckman's treatments were unorthodox. He initially classified influenza and pneumonia as 'jungle fever', which he treated with quinine, and early dysentery with toothpowder as he did not have salts. His treatments improved with experience and after he acquired a stethoscope, scalpel and other implements. But his dentistry remained rudimentary. For much of the time he had only a pair of motor workshop pliers which had to do for forceps. Many of the extractions performed with the pliers ended with the target tooth being crushed. On one occasion Ken Trumble went in to have an infected tooth removed, and he too had the wrong tooth pulled. Eventually a proper pair of forceps was acquired and the standard of camp dentistry improved markedly.

One night after the men had returned from work at the shipyard, one of the English prisoners fell down some steps and dislocated his shoulder. Lloyd Ellerman was present on parade and called for Eyckman to assist. He examined the man's injury and determined he could fix the shoulder. A can of ether from a Red Cross parcel issue was produced. Ellerman poured some over the patient's face while asking him to slowly count to ten. By the time he had reached five, his voice started slurring and he was soon unconscious. Eyckman then went about pushing the shoulder back into place, and after a short while was able to re-set the injury. Once this was done, the patient was carried away from the parade ground and back to the camp medical post. After a few days off work he had recovered sufficiently to return to the shipyard.

If prisoners were too ill to work they were required to report to the administration block where they would be inspected by the Japanese guards. The Japanese medical orderlies, Sleepy and Dopey, would sit in judgment on the presenting prisoners. Mostly the pleas of Eyckman were ignored and the men were ordered to work, even when they were obviously sick, including with severe cases of diarrhoea and dysentery, as Lloyd Ellerman recalled: "The Japanese showed no regard for our welfare and did not care whether we survived or not. This was [e]specially evident in the attitude to, and treatment of, the sick. They were quite inhuman, taking the view that if men were too ill to work then the camp ration would be cut to one third for those not working."[5]

When prisoners were gravely ill they would sometimes be sent to a hospital in Osaka. It could be a rough trip for men who already were suffering, and the treatment that awaited them could be even rougher. Corporal Jack Nicholls was sent to Osaka with severe dysentery: "We were put in the back of an army truck already loaded with an assortment of army items and had to stand for the thirty miles from Kobe to Osaka. The swaying truck, and the bumpy roads, did nothing to help our condition. Imagine trying to take down one's pants in an open truck, as we were passing through thickly populated suburbs, and trying to squat over a bucket! It was an ignominious and embarrassing experience. It was a great relief when the truck stopped, at the sports arena, on the outskirts of Osaka and we were told we had arrived at the hospital."[6]

The hospital was a makeshift clinic built onto the back of a sports ground grandstand which had been covered by hessian that billowed in the breeze and was held in place by timber scantlings. As soon as they arrived, Nicholls and the five other prisoners who had travelled with him on the truck were ordered by the guards to stand to attention for a *tenko* (rollcall). Suddenly, from inside the hospital emerged a Japanese warrant officer dwarfed by a six feet three inches bearded giant who turned out to be Surgeon Commander Jackson, RN, who prior to becoming a POW was in charge of the Hong Kong Naval Hospital. Before that he had been a surgeon at Guy's Hospital, London. He ignored all the Japanese guards, telling the prisoners to come inside and sit down.

Charles Anthony 'Tony' Jackson, an Anglo-Irish officer of the Royal Naval Volunteer Reserve from Surrey, had been captured in Hong Kong on Christmas Day 1941. He would save countless lives while a POW in Japan, often performing essential operations with only old razor and hacksaw blades. At the end of the war he would be honoured with an MBE for his work. The hospital in Osaka where he worked with six English POW orderlies had little or no medical supplies. His wards were bare concrete floors with rows of mats for a capacity of about 60 patients.

Jack Nicholls would marvel at the work Jackson performed:

> The doctor inspired confidence among the patients and staff alike. During our first night, three men died, and the same number the next two nights. At this time I was no better and getting weaker. On the doctor's rounds he gave me a tiny square of chocolate, and on watching this procedure each night, I could see a patient was given chocolate when his condition was bad. He said 'sorry' to me and then, 'we will tell you tomorrow if we think you can make it. I will then give you half a sulphur tablet to see if that

helps'. I survived the night and next morning was given the tablet, the doctor apologising saying half a tablet was all I can spare, as he only had a few left. My diet during the first three days had been barely broth only, and my weight was down to six and a half stone. But by nightfall I had only had two motions, and during the night, none at all. When the doctor came round the next morning he greeted me with a smile, and said, 'It worked!'[7]

That morning seven new prisoners were brought by truck to Jackson's clinic. They had been operated on for hernias at a Japanese hospital and were in a terrible state, as Nicholls witnessed:

There was a mighty shout because all the men were lying on the truck floor, on blankets, soaked in blood and in terrible pain. This was the result of botched surgery and poor sutures. We learnt later that second-year Japanese students from a medical hospital had been allowed to carry out the operations. The doctor demanded needles, sutures and anaesthetic, berating the Japanese. The warrant officer went away and later returned with the supplies demanded. And the doctor took each man in turn and, with the aid of two orderlies, worked all night and until 10am next morning, repairing this damage. Thanks to him and his team, all these men recovered.

After his own recovery, Jack Nicholls returned to the camp at Kobe, where Doug Lush and the other officers assigned him to light duties in the kitchen to help him rebuild his strength. He did such a good job and was so reliable they left him there and put him in charge.

By the start of the war, the Japanese had not signed the Geneva Convention asserting the rights of prisoners of war to humane treatment but Emperor Hirohito had agreed to its provisions. They would be flouted, with monstrous consequences, by his fanatical subjects.

Under the 1929 Convention, officer prisoners were to be detained together and not required to work.

In mid-1943, that situation began to change when about 150 Allied officers were moved from various locations across Japan into Zentsuji camp, located on the island of Shikoku, south-west of Kobe. Among them were a number of the Australian officers from the Kobe camp, but not John Paterson, Ken Trumble or Doug Lush who were determined to stay together with their men in Kobe. When the Japanese told Trumble that he was to be sent to Zentsuji, he appealed to them to let him stay, falsely claiming that he was Lush's cousin. The Japanese relented, agreeing that Trumble could swap places with Lieutenant Johnson, who had been listed to remain. So when the move was made, Johnson instead departed and Trumble stayed.

It would be a fateful decision for Lieutenant Ralph Venn Johnson, a fellow 22nd Brigade headquarters staff officer, from Northbridge in New South Wales. Johnson would survive the deprivations of prison camp life until the very end of the war, only to die on 28 August 1945 – two weeks after the Japanese surrender – when he was crushed by a barrel of relief supplies dropped from an American aircraft over the Zentsuji camp. A bank officer before the war, Johnson had married his nurse sweetheart Florence just days before embarking for Malaya aboard the *Queen Mary* in February 1941.

After the departure of the other officers from Kobe on 31 July 1943, Captain Paterson remained as camp leader with Lush his deputy and adjutant. Aside from Ken Trumble, the camp medico Konrad Eyckman and Dutch army Lieutenant Hendrik Jan Penning were the only other remaining officers.

Language differences would make their task harder. A Dutch prisoner who spoke a little Japanese was nominated to be the prisoners' interpreter. He was brutally treated for his efforts, as Lush explained: "He wasn't fluent and he used to have to hesitate when he got into a bit of a tough spot and he would get a bashing from the guards. So he never really relaxed with the job as he was a bit shy about the whole thing. I don't think he ever told the truth to the guards when we were in a spot of bother but it was the best that we could do." The Japanese had a couple of interpreters who came into the camp. One had been to America and he could speak basic English.

In late July 1943 another 200 British prisoners arrived at the Kobe camp, swelling the numbers to about 600 men. John Paterson would lament how much better the new arrivals had fared in their previous camp in Korea: "At midnight the troops arrived – 200 Englishmen who left Singapore 10 months ago and have been in Korea. In good nick and say they were well treated and plenty of food and Red Cross parcels. I was disappointed as they didn't bring any news."[8]

Like the men under them, the officers grew weaker with the meagre diet and poor conditions in the camp, as Captain Paterson noted in his diary in November 1943 following a serious breakdown in his own health: "Today I did rather a foolish thing, and have paid a severe penalty for it. I played volleyball with Trumble and Lush and caught a chill. Although I changed clothes and took the usual precautions, I didn't feel well at night, and decided to stay in bed – a place which I haven't left for two months having contracted the most severe dose of dysentery we've had in the camp."[9] During his illness, Paterson's weight fell by 15 kilograms.

Chapter 11

HUNGER

Due to physical weakness and malnutrition, we have
four mental cases and dozens of 'punch drunk' men –
men who have reached the non-care stage
through sheer weakness.

John Paterson's Diary[1]

The officers were responsible for managing the food rations each day
while the men were away working at the shipyard. Doug Lush and
Ken Trumble often had to lug huge bags of rice, carried on a pole
slung over their shoulders. Sometimes they and other prisoners not
on work shifts would be sent into the hills surrounding the camp to
gather wood for the boilers. In the early days, the officers were allowed
only half rations, barely enough food to survive. Later their contribution was recognised by the Japanese and they were allowed the same
rations as the men working at the shipyard.

All of the men suffered from the lack of sufficient food and sufficiently nutritious food, especially the bigger men, according to Doug
Lush: "It was the larger framed chaps who were the ones that really
suffered because they needed the extra food as you could realise. A
lot of those blokes were country boys and they had big appetites.
They went down very quickly when they had to live and work on just
a handful of rice."

Food was always scarce and the meagre rations of rice, occasional vegetables and fruit and rare supplements of fish and meat dwindled as the months passed. Lunch for the workers was one and a half small bread buns, which mostly where wolfed down by ravenous men well before lunchtime.

Jack Chapman would describe the rest of the pitiful daily menu:

> The morning and evening meals were usually augmented with a bowl of watery vegetable soup consisting mainly of daikon. It was a long coarse radish type of vegetable with little or no taste but it helped to counter the beri-beri problem. Other vegetables were provided in season but never in great quantities. Whale meat (regarded as a delicacy) was received twice, also fish in the early part of our sojourn. The issue was always small and went into the soup in most cases. Even four or five issues of horse meat were received. As the war came closer to mainland Japan, supplies of extras became less and less until they ceased all together.[2]

At times, the food supply was augmented with food scraps from the nearby naval academy. Doug Lush recalled the 'navy stew' that occasionally was brought to the camp: "It was the scrapings off their plates and you wouldn't believe what was in it. There were cigarette butts and bandages and God knows what. It was the most terrible thing and the blokes were eating this stuff and they were getting diarrhoea. But the Japanese said it was good enough for the POWs and put it into a big tub and sent it out to us. Navy stew came to us about every four or five weeks and we used to announce when it arrived, 'Well, Navy Stew tonight!' and some of the blokes used to jump up and down. I thought I'd try it once and then I couldn't stomach it. When you are hungry you'll eat any damn thing at all."

Lush suffered as much as his fellow prisoners from the lack of adequate food. During his time in captivity he lost almost half his body weight – which dropped from about 85 kilograms to about 48 kilograms. But he believed his general fitness, average build and history of modest eating helped him endure the ordeal better than others.

Once some apples and oranges appeared on the camp menu. After the oranges were distributed, the men were asked by the Japanese to write an appreciation of how they felt about receiving an orange. Lush gathered up the responses: "Most of the blokes wrote, 'We don't want your f-----g orange. You can stick it,' sort of business. 'What we want is food, food, food!' in ever increasing letters. We let a few of those go through because they couldn't trace who wrote them; there were no names on them. But that was the only time we got oranges."

There was a drain at the back of the camp and a small gap in the fencing over the drain left an opening that enabled prisoners to get outside the camp – if they were game enough to risk a bashing, or worse. There were continual dire warnings to prisoners that they should not attempt to escape the confines of the camp. Some ignored them. Robert Ingram, a well-built and energetic 8th Division signaller from Point Clare in New South Wales, was one. Ingram often used the drain exit to sneak out of the camp after dark to scrounge for food. He would steal vegetables from private gardens located nearby. Instead of bringing them back to be cleaned and cooked, he would eat them raw. Ingram either failed to realise or ignored the fact that the gardens were fertilised with excrement from the camp's *benjo* (sewage) cart. If these vegetables were not well boiled they were dangerous to eat.

After one night of foraging outside the fence, Ingram became very ill and later succumbed to toxic poisoning, as Doug Lush recounted: "The poor devil had been working hard every day and was on the point of starving, and these were the risks some of the fellows would take to gain some basic extra weight. It was very sad as he had been one of the most vigorous men we had in camp. He had managed to stay fit, but because he had resorted to going through the drain to procure these vegetables from the outside gardens he instead needlessly died."

The camp quartermaster, civilian guard Ko Nishikawa, was responsible for some of the most vicious assaults on prisoners at Kobe. The 23-year-old had been a watch repairer in Kobe before the war and had served for just one month in the army before being discharged after being wounded on duty – presumably during a training accident. The frustration and humiliation of his short-lived career as a soldier of the Emperor, and his relegation to the demeaning task of minding foreign prisoners, perhaps inflamed the frustration that he would take out on the men under him at Kobe, where he served as camp quartermaster from November 1942 to the end of January 1944.

Nishikawa was both a brute and a thief. He controlled the food supplied to the camp's kitchen and the distribution of the Red Cross parcels – on the very rare occasions that they were distributed. He also was in charge of the camp stores and the issuing of items such as boots. Captain Paterson would have to report to Nishikawa to request replacement boots for those prisoners in need of footwear. It would depend on the guard's mood whether or not he would accede to the requests. And it was well known among the prisoners that Nishikawa was stealing from the camp store and taking food, such as rice, whenever he could.

One day Nishikawa decided to relieve the camp kitchen of a bag of cocoa. He had sneaked the bag to where the drain opening was at the back fence of the camp with the intention, when finishing up for the day, of leaving the camp and making his way around to where he had left the cocoa. Some of the prisoners were aware of his plan and, unbeknown to Nishikawa, had removed the bag from where he had hidden it and returned it to the camp's kitchen. On finding his contraband missing at the end of the day, Nishikawa was furious but he could hardly report the matter to his superiors as he himself had tried to steal the cocoa.

Food remained an obsession for all of the men. "The only thing we ever talked about as prisoners of war was food," Lush recalled. "We didn't talk about women, we didn't talk much about home or anything like that. We talked about food and news, that was about the only thing and, of course, blokes used to write out recipes and that sort of thing to try and satisfy themselves."

Jack Chapman, who like a number of other young prisoners marked his 21st birthday at Kobe – "and still a virgin!" – said fantasies about food totally eclipsed any thoughts of feminine intercourse, social and physical:

> At night time, even during the day at work, certainly on our day off, we talked about nothing but food. We talked about the times at home we used to go to restaurants, the times we had when Sunday was the big lunchtime dinner of the week, the types of meals we had … In civilian life at 22 or 23 years of age, a man wouldn't be thinking consistently, talking continuously about food. He would most certainly be thinking about that three-letter word 'sex' and perhaps doing something about it. Not in our situation, however, we couldn't care less about females or sex. The thought of having any association with passion, any sensuous attachment whatsoever with the female gender, was simply not in our minds.[3]

At the shipyard, desperately hungry men would resort to stealing from the horses stabled nearby, as Mick Kildey explained:

> The soya bean is very rich in vitamins and when everything is extracted from it the residue was turned into a big cake about two feet square and a couple of inches thick, which was used to

feed the horses. It would be nothing to see a bloke sneak away from his job or the lunch room and go to the toilet or something and he would be over stroking the horse on the forehead with one hand and his other hand would be in the horse's tucker bag sneaking a piece of cake out of it and shoving it in his pocket to walk away and eat it later on. It was better than nothing at all.[4]

The normal relationships between officers and the ranks of soldiers were often tested in the hothouse of captivity. The officers were held responsible by the Japanese for maintaining order in the camp and they regularly had to act as intermediaries between the guards and the other prisoners – often a no-win situation. It would be an additional stress for Paterson and the other officers, beyond their own personal daily struggle for survival, as Lush explained:

> Obviously we were trying to get the best deal for the men all the time and if it didn't come about they would go crook and think that we were working with the bloody Japs. It was most unfair. If we had a win, like getting razor blades or concert parties, the blokes would go, 'Oh beauty', but it was a very difficult situation for an officer. We tried to come in between the Japs and the blokes on a number of occasions when there were altercations. Paterson did a good job on those sorts of things and we succeeded to a point but not entirely.

The officers would often use rations of cigarettes and other items to ensure the men's compliance and cooperation. If there was a serious disciplinary problem, the offender would be called into the administration room for a formal hearing. If the offence was upheld, a common punishment was to withhold that prisoner's cigarette ration. The Japanese issued 10 cigarettes a month to all of the prisoners. The loss of the ration was a serious punishment. For smokers, 10 cigarettes was a meagre but vital supply. For non-smokers, cigarettes were a prized trading item.

One of Lush's regular duties was to run the morning parade and *tenko* (rollcall). Leaders of the various sections to which the prisoners were assigned would report back on any issues and concerns among the men. Lush and Trumble would then meet with Paterson after the men had gone to work. They would discuss the condition of the sick, the management of food or preparations for bathing. Then it was time for exercise.

At 10.50 every morning all the men who had not gone to the shipyard would assemble on the parade ground for PT. The Japanese would play music over the camp speakers and Lush would lead 10 minutes of exercise. Even the guards would put down their rifles and join in, as would many of the civilians living nearby the camp. For many of the men, worn down by hunger and illness, it was a struggle, as Lush recalled: "Many of the blokes had lost so much weight they were very lethargic and often would have to sit down. It was rather pathetic. Those that could would have to stand up and do a series of each exercise, numbering up to eight in Japanese. The Japs were all quite serious about it. Even the people outside the camp in the streets would all stop and do these exercises as the music could be heard throughout the community over the loud speakers. It was quite something, even during wintertime."

The men were given two days off work each month. They would work for 15 days straight and then be given a *yasumi*, or rest day. The camp had a bathhouse but there was little coal or other fuel. A few months after the men arrived from Singapore, the Japanese agreed that the officers could go out into the hills to gather firewood. It was, literally, a breath of fresh air for Paterson and his colleagues. As they ranged through the hills collecting fallen branches they would marvel at the village women carrying six or seven logs of wood bundled onto their backs.

The new supply of fuel meant the men were able to take occasional baths. The camp included a large room with a concrete floor, marbled walls, a roof that sloped from one end to the other and a small furnace. In the middle of the room was a small bathing pool. Heating it was a major challenge. The kitchen staff would light the furnace first thing in the morning so by the afternoon when the men returned from the shipyard the pool would be ready. The Japanese expected all the prisoners to share the bath – all 600 of them. The officers insisted that nobody got into the pool until the last of the huts had been through. Each of the men had to have a tin to scoop up water to wash and shave with. Each group had a time limit. As one group came out of the bathroom, the next would go in. When the last group had finished it was open slather, or rather open lather. Dozens of men would jump in and use whatever water was left.

Despite the regular eruptions of violence, Doug Lush had generally good relationships with the guards, who were impressed when they discovered he had been a champion athlete before the war. That respect grew after he organised the first camp sports meeting and took part in the shot-put, broad jump and 50-yards dash, winning them all. Once aware of his sporting prowess, the guards began to challenge him. One day a guard approached Lush on the parade ground and drew a line on the ground:

> He said 'Jump' so I just jumped. He dropped his rifle and bay-
> onet and he jumped and beat me. He didn't realise that I was
> a jumping champion with the Melbourne Harriers. This went
> on three or four times and in the end I thought 'bugger this
> joker' and I jumped and beat him by a mile and he just about
> had a fit. But the upshot was that every six weeks when they
> changed the guards invariably any athletic bloke would come
> over and challenge me. It became a ritual that some bloke with

his rifle would come down and draw a line in the sand and tell me to jump. I gained a certain amount of respect from that and they didn't take it out on me. I purposely never let them win, to keep the upper hand. They were a nation that respected ability, respected truth.

At the first sports meeting, organised on one of the rest days, the men were formed into teams representing the various huts in the camp. The events were modified to take account of the limited resources and the weakened state of the participants. The 100-yard sprint was more like 50 yards and the shot-put was a round rock. A 'Siamese race' was conducted between pairs of men with their legs tied together. Even the modified program tested the stamina of men who had little to spare, as Lush recalled: "The blokes were all so weak it was just impossible to conduct a normal sports meeting. It was a matter of a little burst of energy and then all the fellows were too exhausted to continue. But it was something to do on the rest day to take the men's minds off things for a bit."

The Japanese also had great respect for Paterson who was not only a more senior officer but older than Lush and the other Australian officers: "He was a real officer through and through in many ways and he gained their respect even more by being the number one officer. When Paterson was on parade and when he would address the parade he had presence and I think the Japs recognised him in a different way to me, being 14 years younger than Patto."

At least one guard was sympathetic towards the prisoners. He was an older man with a withered hand who had been in the Japanese navy. While serving aboard the battle cruiser *Ibuki* in 1914 he had helped escort the first convoy of Australian and New Zealand troops across the Indian Ocean to the war in Europe. According to Lush, the guard's only word of English was 'wool': "He would say, 'wool, wool', which meant Australia. But he was the only one who showed a little bit of feeling towards the Australian prisoners. People have asked me whether there were any friendly Japanese guards, and I have said that it wasn't a matter of being friendly; they were trained to be what they were. So they couldn't break away from their orders not to be friendly. Generally the Japanese staff couldn't give a damn about us."

The different nationalities among the prisoners tended to respond differently to the random and often erratic violence of the guards. Doug Lush believed the Dutch and British prisoners tended to be treated more harshly than the Australians, who were more likely to stand their ground when assaulted. He was also convinced that the support Australian prisoners gave each other helped them better survive their ordeal: "What helped Australian POWs was mateship. It didn't apply to the Americans to the same extent, and the Indians didn't have it. Mateship means helping one another and respecting each other. The other nationalities, the Dutch and the British, did not survive to the same extent as the Australians did due to the strength of our code of mateship."

Lush also organised regular quiz sessions to entertain the men and keep their minds off the constant hunger. Sometimes the theme was literature. Other times there were medical questions, or politics and history. Lush prepared the questions after interviewing various prisoners who had areas of special knowledge:

> I kept myself alert by writing in my spare time. When you don't write for years and you don't read, the blokes become just like animals. They're just living to survive and to work. Many of them were really depressed and I could see that when they did eventually get home it would take them a long while to recuperate,

to relearn how to write and read again. That's why I tried to stimulate their minds and get their interest in these things back again while trying to keep morale up.

Lush went to great lengths to establish and maintain his credibility with the guards which, as well as enabling him to intervene successfully when men were being attacked, helped him with the administration of the camp. But it was not enough to save him and the other officers from repeated bashings: "I had about thirty bashings with all sorts of things not withstanding my relationship with the guards. On reflection, I'm very lucky to have got out of it as well as I did. I'm not saying I've got a great constitution, but I've got a reasonably good constitution that sort of kept me going."

On rest days, the Japanese would conduct snap inspections through the camp. While all the prisoners were out on the parade ground, the guards would come through the huts and pick up anything that was being searched for that day. Sometimes it was table knives, other times it was books. The men's greatest fear was losing precious diaries. Hiding places were created under floors and beneath mats. John Paterson stitched the completed pages of his diary into the lining of his jacket.

The men also had various ruses to divert the guards' attention during searches. One was the strategic use of family photos, as Doug Lush explained:

> It was a matter of distracting the Japs all the time and beating them to the punch. If a bloke had photos of his wife and family he would leave them out. The guard would look at the photo on top of the gear whilst not going through the rest of the man's belongings; they were completely distracted. They would pick up a photo and the Jap would ask, 'How many children?', and the bloke would say, 'Ah, ten!' and the Jap would think about this

and then move on to the next man and if he had no photo on top he would instead then go through the gear.

Sometimes Marilyn Monroe played wife to multiple husbands:

In the huts were all these pictures men had been tearing out of papers and magazines. Marilyn Monroe featured prominently on the walls. But when it came time for inspection, down would come Marilyn Monroe and she would go on top of the pile of clothes ready for inspection. Time would be wasted as the guards would do the same thing and everyone would repeat the same thing. There might be ten Marilyn Monroes and she would be all the different men's wife and the bloke would usually say they are married, and they had two children or ten children. It was so farcical.

Chapter 12

VIOLENCE

As I lie in bed thinking of home, lots of little things go
through my mind. I was thinking the other night
of the day I asked Et if I could become engaged,
of the way the baby sang herself to sleep at night,
and of the days at Sassafras.

John Paterson's Diary[1]

They called him Bunny, for reasons lost in time, and he was a larrikin popular with the other 8th Division signallers. Bruce Shirriff
was born and raised in the hamlet of Carcoar, south of Orange in the
central west of New South Wales. He had joined the regular army in
1934, at the age of 19, and was one of the first of the division signallers marched into the Liverpool camp in late July 1940. A clerk and
storeman before enlisting, Shirriff had married his sweetheart, Jean,
a few months before his unit embarked for Malaya.

The reckless and defiant streak that had seen Shirriff repeatedly
punished for being absent without leave during training in Australia
– and busted from corporal back to private – would continue during
his time as a prisoner of war. The consequences would be severe for
him – and for the rest of the men working at the Kawasaki shipyard.

In early August 1943 there was an eruption of violence against
the prisoners at the Kobe camp that would continue for days. It was

111

triggered by a line of graffiti scrawled on a wall in a toilet block at the shipyard, as Jack Chapman recalled: "One of the POWs in camp had light heartedly written on the *benjo* walls some derogatory comments about Kawasaki such as, 'Burn the bloody shipyards down'. This message was seen by our monkey masters and interpreted as a threat of insurrection and all hell broke loose."[2]

As soon as the men returned from work on 8 August 1943 they were ordered onto the parade ground and held for hours as the guards tried in vain to discover who was responsible for the graffiti. It got worse the next night when the men were forced to stay out until after 11pm. Many were taken into the office and roughly interrogated, two of them being put in the guardhouse after a severe bashing. John Paterson noted the severity of the violence in his diary: "This experience was far worse than the first, several men fainting (we were kept standing for six hours). One man who fainted was taken to the regimental aid post where, when he recovered, he was bashed by the medical orderly."[3]

The violence continued the following day when the officers were targeted, driving Paterson close to breaking point. Morimoto inspected the camp and vented his wrath on the camp staff after which his deputy, Sergeant Major Mutsujiro Sakamoto, turned on Lush, Trumble and Penning who were belted with a strap and punched. The ordeal continued into the night, as Paterson wrote: "It was hell. The guards kept me awake all night in their attempts to check the men sleeping in each hut. I was a bundle of nerves and was waiting every minute for something to happen. One of the men told me this morning that I screamed out during the night. I'm not surprised. I'm longing to get away from here. The nervous strain is terrible."[4]

One of the two men held in the guardhouse was Bunny Shirriff, who eventually confessed to scrawling the *benjo* graffiti at the shipyard. He was held for a week, during which time he was given no food, forced to remain silent and given no indication of what his fate would be, as Jack Chapman recounted: "This was perhaps the worst part of any confinement – the lack of any knowledge as to what would happen to you and of course there was no one to whom you could turn for help. However, seven days later he was released and came back to the hut, red eyed, very stressed and extremely hoarse, hardly able to speak. This may have been due to the extreme nervous reaction, but fortunately he did recover after a short space of time and some preferred treatment by the kitchen. No broken bones, no broken spirit."[5] For his part in the bashing of Shirriff and Warrant Officer Mulcahy, Sergeant Major Sakamoto was sentenced to three years hard labour by the US Eighth Army Military Commission that conducted war crimes trials after the Japanese surrender.

The relationship between the men and the guards was always tense, as bashings were frequent and random. Sometimes they were triggered by the most trivial things. Even happiness was forbidden, as Paterson recorded: "A Jap doctor called again today and bashed people right, left and centre for not saluting him. Very edifying for an officer. The cooks were singing and whistling in the kitchen and he bashed them for that and issued an order against any whistling or singing (or happiness of any kind)."[6]

The violence was a constant threat for all prisoners, including Doug Lush: "They would bash you if they felt like it but it was also in their minds that they needed our blokes to work. When we came into the camp, the guards didn't give a damn if they knocked us over or anything but suddenly Morimoto would order them lay off as they would have to provide so many men to work the next day. The guards in the camps were moderate; some good and some not so good. If the blokes did something wrong in their eyes they would get a bashing, there's no doubt about that. If you walked around just whistling you would get a belting. Or for smiling or singing a song. If a Jap guard was going by, he would just come over and whack you."

On more than one occasion Colonel Sotaro Murata, the commanding officer for all of the POW camps in the Osaka region, would take part in the assaults on prisoners. Once he lost his temper after arriving at the Kobe camp and discovering that the toilets were overflowing – despite repeated appeals to the guards from Paterson and the other officers to have them emptied, as Lush recalled: "The colonel came in and he saw the overflow and he blamed the Japanese officer. But he blamed us too so he came up to us and he took his belt off and he belted us. When we got back we were smarting so we got to the interpreter and we told him to go up and tell them we had already notified them about the overflow and we were not to blame. Well he went up there and told them and lo and behold we got another belting."[7]

Jack Chapman recounted the favourite methods of sadistic violence employed by some of the Japanese and Korean guards:

> Heavy poles were popular and perhaps the favourite, pick handles and rifle butts were also up there with the best and boots and fists made up the range. The poor unfortunate victim in most instances would be stood strictly to attention by the guard or guards and then the 'fun' would begin. If the poor POW refused to go down, the pounding became worse, and if he did the boots and butts would come into play. Broken ribs and limbs suffered received no medical attention and were left to heal as best they could, naturally whilst still going out to work unless John Paterson or one of our other officers could wrangle something. One favourite pastime of the guards was to stand one of us to attention as punishment for something allegedly done, hands over his head

holding a couple of house bricks or something similar and left there all night or day. No lowering of arms or otherwise resting, or another brick would be added.[8]

The gratuitous violence also was a constant theme when the men were working at the shipyard, not only from the guards but also from some of the other Japanese workers, according to Mick Kildey: "Some of the workforce in the shipyard were young Japanese – I presume they'd been students and were pulled out to go into the workforce because they were very young. And when they saw the brutality of the Japanese guards and our bosses, they decided they'd try a little bit out as well. So the result was that no matter what age the Jap was, he had the right to give you a thumping whenever he felt like it. Each day was a struggle."[9]

Some of the worst violence was meted out by the Korean guards. As increasing numbers of young Japanese men were conscripted to fight, their places in tasks such as prison camp guarding were taken over by Korean workers, as Jack Chapman recalled:

> We landed so many of them, evidently all the dregs from Korea. We had one beauty, a big heavy brute of a bloke, no brains, lots of brawn and we named him Joe Louis after arguably the greatest heavyweight boxer of our times, an American who fought around the 1930s and 1940s. There were others, The Snoop and The Snake, but all were sub human. I was on the receiving end of some sparring practise with Joe Louis at one time for some trivial offence that now escapes me. Maybe I looked straight at him. 'Don't make eye contact, Jack,' I used to say to myself, 'Don't make eye contact!' But I did, didn't I![10]

As the months of imprisonment wore on, many of the sick and starving prisoners abandoned the struggle to survive, as Doug Lush lamented: "Some of the young blokes just gave up; they lost their will to live. And it was pretty hard when a bloke had made up his mind. You would give them a pat on the back and attempt to encourage them, to try and turn these fellows around, but it would depend on how far they'd gone. When you gave encouragement to these depressed men and got a positive response, it was pretty rewarding."

One POW renowned for the ability to draw his mates out of their depression was Freddie Brown, a private with the 2/18th Battalion from Kempsey, New South Wales. Des Mulcahy would praise Brown's skills as an "uneducated psychologist": "Freddie had a knack with people. If I saw one of the blokes starting to get a bit down in the dumps, a bit morose, I would say to Fred, 'Fred I think so and so could do with a half hour of your talk, would you go down and have a yarn with him?' Freddie would go down and sit down with this bloke and before you could say Jack Robinson, he had him laughing and joking … He was absolutely fantastic the way he could get these blokes out of their mood, getting them back up on their feet again."[11]

One of those who could not be encouraged to fight on was George Powell, a 32-year-old lance sergeant with the 8th Division Signals. Born in Brisbane, Powell had worked as a printing compositor before enlisting in Sydney, where he left behind his wife Ethel and a young daughter when the division embarked for Malaya. One morning in March 1944, Powell came to John Paterson and told him simply, "I don't think I can go on, sir". Paterson pleaded with the guards for Powell to be excused from work that day. The response was emphatic, "No, Work!", as Doug Lush recounted: "Powell returned from his shift at the shipyards that day and just died. He was worked to death, basically. It affected Captain Paterson greatly, as he had tried hard to save Powell."

New recruit: Lieutenant J.F.D. Lush, Royal
Australian Corps of Signals.
(Credit: Stewart Lush)

Captain John Paterson: his courageous
leadership would help save many lives in the
Kobe prison camp.
(Credit: Janet Paterson)

Dashing: Doug Lush at Albert Park, Melbourne c.1937. His athleticism would be admired by the
Japanese and help him endure captivity.
(Credit: Stewart Lush)

Private First Class Willem Wilsterman: starved, tortured and frozen to death at the Kobe camp in December 1943.
(Credit: Wilsterman family)

Lieutenant Ken Trumble in Sydney before embarking for Malaya in 1941.
(Credit: Hugh & Michael Trumble)

Corporal Harold Stephen 'Mick' Kildey, 2/10 Field Ambulance: Survivor of Kobe and Fukuoka.
(Credit: Deborah Kelly)

Private Lloyd Ellerman, 8th Division Signals: his lost secret prison camp diary was found and returned by British occupation forces after the war.
(Credit: Peter Ellerman)

Jack and Bob Chapman: the brothers enlisted, fought and were captured together
– and ensured each other's survival.
(Credit: Peter Chapman)

Tomas 'Spud' Murphy: the 15-year-old who lied
about his age to go to war and lived to tell the tale.
(Credit: *The Age*)

Warrant Officer Des Mulcahy: the larrikin leader
of POWs at the Kawasaki shipyard.
(Credit: Australians at War Archive)

Brigadier Harold Taylor and his 22nd Brigade Headquarters staff, Port Dickson, Malaya, April 1941. Doug Lush is in the back row, third from the left; and Lieutenant Ralph Johnson (killed in an accident after the Japanese surrender) is in the back row, far left.
(Credit: Stewart Lush)

Staff of the Australian Army Nursing Service, 2/4th Casualty Clearing Station, in Singapore on 20 January 1942, a month before the city fell to the Japanese. Only one would survive the war.
Back row, from left: Jess Dorsch (drowned Banka Island 14 February 1942), Peggy Wilmott (executed Banka Island beach 16 February 1942), Mina Raymont (died of illness, Sumatra 8 February 1945), Elaine Balfour-Ogilvy (executed Banka Island) and Peggy Farmaner (executed Banka Island).
Front row: Shirley Gardam (died of illness, Sumatra 4 April 1945), Matron Irene Drummond (executed Banka Island) and Mavis Hannah (survived the sinking of the SS *Vyner Brooke* and three years as a POW).
(Credit: John Delmore Emmett, Australian War Memorial 120518)

The Fall Guy: Lieutenant General Arthur Percival surrenders Singapore to General Tomoyuki Yamashita, 15 February 1942 – Saburo Miyamoto.
(Credit: Saburo Miyamoto / National Museum of Modern Art, Tokyo)

16 Adam Park: From grand British colonial residence to Japanese prison camp.
(Credit: The Adam Park Project)

The trophy for the 1942 Melbourne Cup Frog Race, made from a coconut shell and scrap metal by prisoners at Adam Park.
(Credit: Australian War Memorial 31985)

The *Kamakura Maru* arrives in Yokohama in late 1942 with the ashes of six Japanese sailors killed in the midget submarine raid on Sydney Harbour. The ship had earlier unloaded the prisoners of C Force in Nagasaki.
(Credit: Shashin Shuho / Wikimedia Commons)

Signaller Bob Mitchell with his sister Nell Ctercteko, in Sydney in 1941. Mitchell began sketching as a POW and would become a noted artist after the war.
(Credit: Suzanne and Gordon Alexander)

The Kobe Camp: Osaka 5-D Prisoner of War Camp (Maruyama, Kobe), from the secret sketchpad of Robert Boyed Mitchell (Signaller Bob Mitchell, from Marrickville, NSW).
(Credit: Suzanne & Gordon Alexander)

Captain Paterson leads the funeral service for Lance Corporal Robert Flanagan who died in May 1942 after falling from a ship's bow at the Kawasaki shipyard.
(Credit: Stewart Lush)

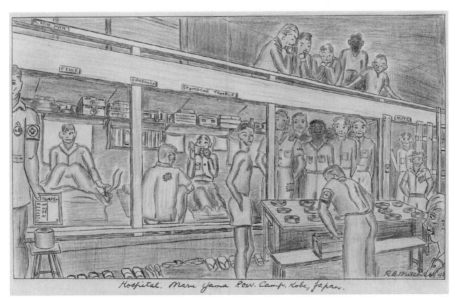

The hospital hut at the Kobe camp – Robert Boyed Mitchell.
(Credit: Suzanne & Gordon Alexander)

The Kawasaki shipyard, Kobe, April 1940.
(Credit: Pinterest)

Prisoners and civilians at work at the Kawasaki shipyard – Robert Boyed Mitchell.
(Credit: Suzanne & Gordon Alexander)

Raining Fire: American B-29 Superfortress bombers shower incendiaries over Kobe Harbour in early June 1945. The raids would raze the Kawasaki shipyard and much of the city.
(Credit: US Air Force)

Fukuoka Camp 26: After the Kobe firebombing, the POWs were sent to work in the deadly Yoshikuma coal mine.
(Credit: 2/4th Machine Gun Battalion)

Australian POWs at work in the Yoshikuma coal mine – Robert Boyed Mitchell.
(Credit: Suzanne & Gordon Alexander)

Liberation: Australian POWs at Fukuoka Camp 26 photographed on 15 August 1945 – the day Japan surrendered. The Chapman brothers stand towards the right in the middle row, Jack in a slouch hat, and Bob nearby in peaked cap. Lloyd Ellerman is on the far left in the back row. Tom Murphy is also in the back row, fifth from the left.
(Credit: Australian War Memorial P03541.009)

Relief: Prisoners welcome US Air Force food relief drops from the rooftops of the Fukuoka camp – Robert Boyed Mitchell.
(Credit: Suzanne & Gordon Alexander)

About Face: Colonel Sotaro Murata, commander of POW camps in the Osaka/Kobe region, after his arrest in August 1945, with Australian Lieutenant John Fuller and US Army Captain John Riley. Murata would be sentenced to life imprisonment for war crimes.
(Credit: Australian War Memorial 019397)

'Bonnie Leslie': Australian Lieutenant John Fuller removes the sword of Captain Yasuji Morimoto, Kobe camp commander, after his arrest in August 1945. Morimoto would be sentenced to 40 years' imprisonment for war crimes.
(Credit: Australian War Memorial 019396)

Free man: Captain John Paterson tours the ruins of Osaka in September 1945.
(Credit: Australian War Memorial 019380)

Homeward Bound: Former Australian POWs on route to Sydney aboard the aircraft carrier HMS *Formidable*. Captain Paterson stands on the left side.
(Credit: Peter Ellerman)

Jubilant relatives crowd the wharf at Circular Quay in Sydney to welcome home 1300 former Eighth Division POWs aboard HMS *Formidable*, 13 October 1945.
(Credit: Ern McQuillan)

HMS *Formidable* docked at Sydney's Circular Quay after repatriating POWs from Manila, 13 October 1945.
(Credit: Ern McQuillan)

Above: Ken Trumble (right) greets his twin brother Robert at Melbourne's Spencer Street Station after arriving by train from Sydney. Army officials staged the surprise reunion without telling either man.
(Credit: Hugh & Michael Trumble)

Left: Lieutenant Colonel Franklin M. Fliniau, the senior Allied officer at Ikuno POW camp whose chance meeting after the Japanese surrender saved interpreter Kazuo Kobayashi from imprisonment.
(Credit: US-Japan Dialogue on POWS)

First Lieutenant Oel Johnson survived the Bataan Death March and three years as a POW in Japan.
(Credit: Olinda Major)

Civvie Street: Lloyd Ellerman back in Sydney, October 1945.
(Credit: Peter Ellerman)

Former prison guard Sergeant Yoshinari Minemoto, wrongly jailed for war crimes, and former POW camp interpreter Kazuo Kobayashi in 1988.
(Credit: Olinda Major)

Reunited: Frank Fliniau and his wife welcome Kazuo Kobayashi to their home in Wildwood, California, in 1988.
(Credit: US-Japan Dialogue on POWS)

Wedding Day: Doug Lush and Elsa Clarke depart Wesley Church after their marriage in Melbourne in 1952.
(Credit: Stewart Lush)

Last Post: John Frederick Douglas Lush, the last surviving officer of the 22nd Brigade, leads the 2004 Anzac Day march in Melbourne.
(Credit: Stewart Lush)

Powell died on Paterson's 40th birthday. The captain was awoken at 3.30am to be given the news. That night he chronicled his despair at the loss of yet another young Australian life: "Poor Powell. I'd been trying to protect him as much as possible and had him in camp for a month, but had to send him out again this month. He was worked to a standstill; collapsed at the shipyards yesterday and was brought home on a stretcher, but was semi-conscious and just faded away. He left such a nice little baby girl – I have his wallet and photographs."[12]

The Japanese were unmoved. They remained emphatic and unwavering in their credo "No work; no eat", as Doug Lush attested: "That was it in a nutshell, whether you were working on building a submarine or no matter what. There's the job and if you don't do it you don't eat and that was it – and you would possibly incur a bashing at the same time. So it was one way all of the time, as far as the Japs were concerned. They were the masters and we just had to do these things and if the men couldn't take it that was what would happen. There were two or three suicides at Kawasaki whilst I was there."

When a prisoner died, those that survived did their best to provide a dignified funeral for them. One of the officers would say a prayer before all the men assembled on parade. The unenviable task of removing the body for cremation generally then fell to Corporal Blues, one of the medical orderlies who worked with the camp doctor, Konrad Eyckman. After a funeral service had concluded, Blues would collect the body and place it in one of the large barrels in which bean curd occasionally was delivered to the camp. He would then load the barrel on a trolley and it would be wheeled down to the nearby crematorium.

The Japanese guards might have tolerated the prisoner funerals, but often their disrespect for the dead, as for the living, would disgust the men, including Lloyd Ellerman: "I have never forgotten one degrading incident. It involved all POWs on the parade ground outside the hospital hut. We were waiting to pay our last respects to one of our comrades being taken away for cremation. The vehicle used was a small handcart. While we stood to attention, an armed Japanese guard thought it was very amusing to loll on the cart and to grin derisively at us."[13]

Chapter 13

NEWS

Both well, conditions good but be pleased to get home
to Long Bay.

Card sent from Kobe POW camp by Jack and Bob Chapman
to their parents in Sydney[1]

In April 1944 there was pandemonium at the Kobe camp after two British prisoners escaped – despite the impossible odds of them surviving undetected for long in an alien country, let alone fleeing the Japanese islands and making their way back to Allied lines. It was an especially reckless move given it was well known that the routine Japanese response to escape attempts was the immediate execution of those who tried. Infamously, four Australian POWs had been executed by firing squad for attempting to flee Singapore in August 1942.

Charles Rodaway and another prisoner named Smith had made their break on the night of 16 April, some time after returning from the day shift at the shipyard. They took with them a few small loaves of bread and an obsolete map of the area. John Paterson recorded the dramatic event in his diary: "Quite sensational! Two Englishmen escaped last night. The men didn't go to work today. We remained on the parade ground all day and search parties were organised with BL [Bonnie Leslie/Morimoto] and Colonel Murata supervising operations ... There are many strange faces in the camp including a lot of officers."[2]

119

Rodaway had joined the Loyal (North Lancashire) Regiment before being posted to Shanghai in 1934. He was transferred to Singapore in 1938 and after the fall of the city was one of the British prisoners sent to work at the Kawasaki shipyard. Ken Trumble discovered that he and Smith had fled while doing the evening rollcall at the Kobe camp on 17 April. Doug Lush marvelled at their audacity, and folly: "When you're in Japan where can you go without any food and when you stand out so obviously within the community? Well, they were free for about three days before they were picked up – without any shoes on so they couldn't run away again. They beat them up a bit and put them in the guardhouse."

Jack Chapman remembers the moment the prisoners were brought back to the camp: "The unfortunate two escapees were still dressed in their POW clothing with their hands tied behind their backs with barbed wire ... I remember looking at them on the parade ground, looking at these two young people being led away by those sub human monsters – so degrading, so pitiful – and at the time wondering what sort of life was in front of them over the coming months and years."[3]

Colonel Murata warned the assembled prisoners of dire consequences if others attempted to escape, then bizarrely ended his speech by declaring: "After the darkness and hardship, comes the happiness."[4] But there would be no happiness for any of the prisoners, and only darkness and hardship for Rodaway and Smith. Enraged by the escape, the Japanese cut further the already pitiful daily rations of all the prisoners and stepped up security, with the Australian officers forced to do regular checks on prisoner numbers throughout the nights.

After being led away from the parade ground, Rodaway and Smith were blindfolded and lined up before a firing squad. "I said to my pal, 'This is it'," Rodaway said later. But at the last moment the officer in charge ordered the firing squad to shoulder arms and marched them away. The pair was later sentenced to 15 years detention at Sakai Prison in Osaka. Rodaway would later describe the horrendous conditions in which they were held: "There was no heat or fan; no water, a wooden pail for a toilet, one light hung from the ceiling, a small barred window at the rear of the cell. Clothing was one thin shirt, one thin trousers, no shoes or socks, no jacket or kimono. No wooden box, only the floor to sit on. Only one thin blanket for cover. Bathing was usually allowed once a month; no soap, no washcloth or towel, no clean clothing."[5]

Rodaway and Smith would be freed a week after the Japanese surrender in August 1945.

By chance, Des Mulcahy would play a role in their liberation. A few months before the surrender, Mulcahy, who was in Osaka with a medical party, had been walking past the building where the prisoners were being held, accompanied by a civilian guard: "I asked him what the big building was and he said it was a jail. He said, 'There are two Englishmen in there.' I pricked my ears up straight away. I said, 'Two Englishmen?' He said, 'Yes'. When the war ended, I notified the authorities that there were two prisoners of war at that camp and they went and found them. They had virtually been held in solitary confinement in the dark all the years … They were in a terrible mess. They shot the two Japanese guards and they took the blokes away."[6]

Rodaway's family was stunned when he arrived home in Blackpool, having read reports in the local paper that he had been killed. Despite the trauma of his time in Japan, he would migrate soon after the war to Canada where he died in August 2017 at the age of 101.

Just east of the port of Kobe was the site of the 19th-century foreign concession – a grand European enclave where American, British and other foreign merchants had built their businesses and opulent homes, and enjoyed exemption from Japanese laws and administration, after the country opened to trade with the West in 1868. While the concession had been returned to Japanese control in 1899, throughout World War II it remained the neighbourhood in which many residents from the Axis powers and neutral countries lived.

The lingua franca of the expatriate community was English and they received daily copies of newspapers, including the venerable *Mainichi Shimbun*, in English, which revealed a lot of details about the war even if through a partisan lens. Private Ken Collins, one of Mick Kildey's mates from the 2/10 Field Ambulance, struck a secret deal with one of the Japanese shipyard workers that would throw a lifeline to the news-starved prisoners at the Kobe camp, as Kildey explained:

> He used to get the newspaper about once a week and he would put it under his crutch. The Japs were reluctant to feel around that area when they were searching you. I think they had an inferiority complex. The paper was taken back to camp and read by a person in each hut and the news would be relayed so that everyone in the camp knew what was going on except the Japs. It was fair dinkum news of the war and they knew every blow that was being struck. They even got news of the Battle of Stalingrad in Russia and the different island conquests as the Americans and Australians fought their way through the islands.[7]

Other prisoners also managed to smuggle English-language papers into the camp, including Harold Fischer, a Victorian signaller and fearless scrounger who had obtained and operated one of the radio sets hidden at the Adam Park camp back in Singapore. Fischer worked in the foundry at the shipyard, as Lloyd Ellerman recounted: "It wasn't long before he had a civilian worker on side to provide him with English-language newspapers – either the *Nippon Times* or the *Mainichi Times* … There was a group of five of us, all non-smokers, so we used our meagre cigarette ration to bribe the civilian. Harold took all the risk bringing the papers in, and this went on for some 18 months. After lights out we used to study the newspaper … We'd have one about every week."[8]

The men craved news of the world beyond their prison and particularly information about the course of the war. When copies of the paper were not available, the men had to rely on fragments of information gleaned from Japanese workers and guards, but they often were unreliable sources, according to Lush: "When you spoke with some of the Japs about the news, they would say, 'We are bombing Australia', and of course some of the blokes would take them on and say, 'Oh, you've bombed Australia, so have you bombed Sydney?' And the Jap would say, 'Yes, bomb, bomb'. And another would ask, 'Have you bombed Timbuktu?' And the Jap would say, 'Yes, bomb, bomb, bomb'."

The secret knowledge that the tide of war was turning in the Allies' favour and that victory seemed only a matter of time would sustain men who had every other reason to despair of their fate, as Jack Chapman reflected:

> Bob and I never lost our feeling of optimism, an attitude that was shared right throughout the camp, even if in varying degrees. I suppose it was just human nature. It was an attitude that certainly did contribute to our health and mental stability. Our irreversible thought was that we would be going home one day and free from all the military control, back to civilian life and all that was good in Australia. These poor bloody blokes here in uniform when defeated would be going back into civilian life with all the hardships and severity of a conquered country.[9]

More than information about the progress of the war, the men craved news of home and their loved ones. Their anguish about whether their families even knew where they were was compounded by the knowledge that those back in Australia were also suffering from the uncertainty about their fate and, worse, the likelihood that many parents, siblings, wives and sweethearts would have presumed they were dead.

Lloyd Ellerman and the other Australian prisoners at Kobe received their first mail from home on 9 April 1944 – more than two years after they had been taken prisoner. They were first allowed to write home – and then only a heavily censored 12-word card – in June 1943:

> We were delightfully inundated with mail after the end of the hostilities – clear evidence that mail was deliberately withheld at the time. Younger generations reading this story may not realise the heartache and endless worry, indeed the whole burden, which rested with loved ones at home. From the start of captivity (15 February 1942) it took the Japanese until 21 June 1943 to release the list in which my name was included. The delays in releasing mail meant the same anguish at home. While gratefully received, it only meant that the sender was alive at the time of writing, usually 12 months or more beforehand.[10]

The Japanese had an appalling record of providing even basic information about the 32,000 POWs held in camps in Japan and the many more imprisoned across other parts of Asia. Despite the stipulations of the Geneva Conventions, the Japanese did not provide timely and detailed lists of the POWs in their hands to the Allied authorities, blocked direct access to prisoners by the International Red Cross and permitted few prison camp visits by Red Cross officials. When those visits were allowed, the Japanese went to great lengths to give a false impression that their captives were being treated humanely and not being starved, beaten and denied access to proper medical care.

According to the British Forces War Records website, the Allied authorities were relentless in seeking detailed information from the Japanese about the fate of Allied nationals in their hands, facilities for the sending of relief supplies and mail, and permission for neutral inspectors to visit POW and internment camps. Despite repeated requests for the regular forwarding of complete lists, not only of captures but of transfers and casualties, the Japanese appear never to have set up an organisation capable of dealing even with the notifications of capture of the 300,000 Allied nationals in their hands. The first British lists did not come through until May 1942; by January 1943 less than a quarter had been notified, and by September 1943 only 65 per cent of the British prisoners of war and only 20 per cent of the civilians. On average, New Zealand next-of-kin waited 18 months for the first news of their prisoner or internee relative.[11]

The Japanese were similarly indifferent – and callous – about mail. Besides that sent on exchange ships, mail for prisoners of war in the Far East was by July 1942 being transported across Russia to her Pacific seaboard and then to Japan, under an agreement reached with the Soviet government. The distribution of this mail among the prisoner of war and internment camps in Japan and Japanese occupied territory was slow and haphazard.[12]

Piles of undelivered mail were found in some Japanese camp offices on liberation, and it is believed some was destroyed to avoid the work involved in censorship. The amount of mail received varied greatly for the hundreds of POW camps scattered across Asia. One New Zealander who worked on the Thai–Burma railway received 126 letters, another only three. Prisoners in Japan on the whole fared better than those in the Dutch East Indies where the number seldom reached double figures. New Zealanders at Macassar received no mail at all.

The average number of cards which the Japanese allowed to be sent out was between four and five for the whole period of captivity, and only some of these reached their destinations.

Occasionally, the prisoners at Kobe camp were permitted to write brief letter cards to their families. While the messages were censored and the men were sceptical of the prospects of them ever reaching their destination, it was at least a chance of making contact with home, as Jack Chapman recalled:

> It was a constant concern to us that our folks back home may have no idea of our whereabouts, certainly of our health, and in our case whether Bob and I were still together. We had been able to send a card home from Kawasaki earlier on, a limit of about 12 words that were heavily censored by the Japanese. We wrote something along the lines of, 'Both well, conditions good but be pleased to get home to Long Bay'. We did not know at the time of course if this letter card would get through to Australia but on returning home in 1945 we found that Pearly and Dad had received it.[13]

In June 1944 there was a changing of the guard at the Kobe camp. 'Bonnie Leslie' (Lieutenant Yasuji Morimoto) was promoted to captain and given charge of several POW camps in the Kobe/Osaka area. The new commandant was Lieutenant Kokichi Asokawa. To the astonishment of Mick Kildey and the rest of the Australians, Asokawa spoke fluent English and declared that he had previously lived at Pymble on Sydney's north shore. He invited some of the prisoners to dinner in the camp which raised pleasant expectations until it was specified that the guests would need to bring their own food. Asokawa asked each of the men who attended where they came from and he appeared to know about all of the places they mentioned, which impressed Kildey:

"He was quite a pleasant bloke and things were a bit easier in the camp during his stay. He brought in some orange coloured powder and gave it to us, paid for out of our ten sen a day wages. It was orange powder ground from orange peel. It probably had some vitamin C in it, but not enough."[14]

In late 1944 several of the men at the Kobe camp were given a rare and priceless opportunity to send a voice message home that would confirm, at least, that they were still alive. They were taken to a local radio station on the outskirts of Kobe and allowed to record a 40-word message that would be broadcast from Tokyo on 31 December.

One of the chosen few was Lloyd Ellerman: "Presumably the Red Cross was able to give appropriate warning as my mother heard the message. It was garbled and had a couple of Christian names thrown in which had no relation to our family and friends. However, it meant a lot to know in December 1944 that I was alive only four weeks before. They would have taken my own words with a grain of salt. Fancy me saying that I was 'in good health and excellent spirits' also 'I am in good hands and all is well'. Nothing could have been further from the truth really – but we wanted to give the message every chance of going through."[15]

Three months later, Ellerman received a telegram from his mother, via Geneva and Tokyo, that made his heart soar: "Delighted Receive Radio December".

Chapter 14

SANTA

Then one day the Yanks will relieve us,
Arriving in all sorts of crafts.
In a rickshaw I'll drive round old Kobe
With a little Nip boy in the shafts.

Popular verse from a concert in the Kobe camp[1]

Christmas 1944 – two years after the men arrived at Kobe – was a turning point. The Japanese gave permission for the first concert to be staged in the camp. The prisoners interpreted this uncharacteristic concession as confirmation that the tide of the war was turning in the Allies' favour and the Japanese were softening the hardline stance towards their captives.

The request for the concert party was made by Doug Lush, who thought the chances of approval were slim. He was astonished when the Japanese interpreter returned the next day declaring that the prisoners had permission: "The blokes were pretty much exhausted and the Japanese interpreter, who was a no hoper, came out and said that the next day we could 'beat the drum'. The permission coincided with a decision to allow a rare distribution of the many Red Cross parcels being held in the camp store."

The men were supposed to receive one Red Cross parcel per month, but while they starved the Japanese either refused to release them or stole many for their own use. According to Lush, in more than three years the prisoners received fewer than seven parcels. When they were distributed, the prisoners usually had to share one box between two or three men. For Christmas 1944, there would be one parcel between several men.

In a further effort to lift morale, Lush decided he would play Santa for the men and dress up for the Red Cross parcel distribution. Mick Kildey was deeply impressed, as were many others: "Lieutenant Lush dressed up as Santa Claus (just where the hell he got the suit from I do not know) surrounded by this mound of boxes and he was shouting 'Merry Christmas'. When the rollcall was over, we filed by one by one and took a box. It was the best and only piece of enjoyment we had during our stay in that camp – other than when we saw the Japs bashing one another up."[2]

Lush's Santa suit was tailored by one of the prisoners from a red blanket owned by a POW who had died. White filling from the Canadian Red Cross parcels was stitched around the edges of the suit. A pair of long boots was loaned by one of the Dutch prisoners. When the men returned from the shipyard that night, Lush was ready and waiting: "I remember bringing tears to a couple of the blokes' eyes as I handed out those Red Cross parcels. They had come back from the shipyards and they were weary from the work. The Dutch were very sentimental; a lot of them had taken their children's clothes with them to remind them of their families."

The star of the first concert was a ventriloquist's doll that Lush had made from tissue and toilet paper and dressed in some of the Dutch children's clothes. Lush's act delighted the prisoners and astonished the Japanese, who had never seen such a thing: "We had it well rehearsed. I would talk to the doll and say, 'So you're Gerry Gee', and this bloke crouching under the table behind a curtain would answer back, 'Yes, I'm Gerry Gee'. The Japs just about jumped out of their skins as they thought this bloody doll was really talking. My problem, of course, was to be able to get this bloke out from underneath the table without them seeing. So I would have all the lights quickly turned off and a few minutes later, after the lights had been restored, I would say on stage, 'Oh well, that's the end for tonight' and with that I would lift off the curtain from the table and there would be no-one there."

Lush took control of planning for that and subsequent concerts and adopted the title "C.B. Cochran Presents" for his productions. Sir Charles Blake Cochran, generally known as C.B. Cochran, was an English theatrical manager and impresario who produced some of the most successful musical revues, musicals and plays of the 1920s and 1930s, and was a close associate of Noël Coward. Kobe's Cochran would screen prospective talent: "I would interview the men to discover what they could do. A bloke would say that he could sing so I would say, 'OK show us what you can do'. I would sit back there and this bloke would then sing a song. The next one I might interview for the chorus, which was supposed to be four girls. I would say, 'Bring them on', and then they would all come out on stage dressed as girls – with tennis balls cut in half concealed as boobs. I would have to sit back there and control everything on stage."

Ken Trumble made a unique contribution. He fashioned a piece of pinewood into an old-fashioned microphone which he attached to a couple of pieces of wire to create a frame. He would 'broadcast' from one side to another prisoner and do a talk-back for the audience, again to the bemusement of the Japanese. Some Dutch prisoners made ukuleles in the camp and Trumble made a triangular guitar and negotiated with the guards to acquire some strings. Other instruments were sourced through the guards. Lush managed to negotiate the purchase of a trombone, a clarinet and a violin: "We had only one Englishman who could play a trombone and the only thing he could play was 'In the Mood' by Glenn Miller. And so we had 'In the Mood' played at us morning, noon and night."

Lush encouraged the men to maintain personal standards and his efforts would unwittingly earn him the lasting respect of the Japanese. He promoted regular shaving both as a means of keeping up appearances and keeping morale up, but the men would complain that they didn't have razor blades. So Lush approached the senior guards and asked whether a box of razor blades could be purchased using some of the workers' daily allowances.

Soon after making the request, Lush was called the administration building. He had ordered 50 – *goji-tsu* – and a box containing the blades was handed over to him. When he went back to his hut he counted the blades and discovered there were 51: "I didn't think for a moment that it was a trick because most of the Japs couldn't count. Anyhow, I bundled them all up again and I went back and I said, 'I wanted fifty, goji-tsu not goji-ichi'. So I counted them up, five, ten, fifteen, twenty and I had three or four of them there trying to count. It was quite amusing. The extra blade was then given back to them."

The guards were impressed and thereafter Lush had a reputation for integrity that paid dividends for him and many of his fellow prisoners:

> I got a name for being very honest. When the Japs had an alter-
> cation or something and Lush spoke, they would believe Lush.
> It really helped me but it also really helped the camp. It was a
> very simple thing, childish you might say, but it certainly had an
> impact. From then on, if a bloke was being thrashed because he'd

been caught pinching salt I would say, 'What's the matter with this bloke?' and the Jap would say, 'Man stealing the salt down at the shipyards'. Then I would say to the Jap, 'This man wasn't stealing the salt, he found it'. The Jap would reply, 'Ah, found it' and stop hitting the chap.

But there were limits to this state of grace. None of the officers were immune from the periodic, random and often severe beatings that were a constant element of life in the Kobe camp. Lush and John Paterson were frequently bashed, especially by the burly and brutish Sergeant Major Sakamoto. Often the violence was in response to the actions of others beyond their control. Once Paterson was punched in the jaw by Sakamoto because the other officers had been found asleep during the afternoon. A few days later he was "knocked down and struck again" by Sakamoto – after complaining to Lieutenant Morimoto about the earlier assault.

If Paterson struggled at times to be treated by the Japanese with the respect due to the most senior of the Allied officers, he earned it from the men for his selfless efforts to improve their miserable living conditions, as Lush affirmed: "Paterson was the authority. He still had his cap and jacket, so he stood out as the number one man. Everywhere he went, the troops recognised him and would salute him. So he did a fair job as far as the dignity of the position controlling the camp was concerned. The newly rotated guards used to always come around to see who he was."

Between the intermittent episodes of conflict and abuse, life in the camp was built around mundane and monotonous daily rituals. The officers had to negotiate with the Japanese over rations and there was rollcall twice a day, morning and night. All the prisoners would be required to line up in their sections on the parade ground to be counted off.

There was also a fire picket each night. The officers had to prepare a roster and each section had to nominate a number of men for the guard duty. The rostered prisoners were required to report to Lush at 1am each morning and at further intervals through the night.

There were persistent challenges for the officers dealing with theft, particularly of food. Once a prisoner was caught after stealing a Red Cross parcel. The guards complained to Lush that the storeroom had been broken into and several parcels were missing: "All hell broke loose. A search was made and the parcels could not be found anywhere. We looked in every place we knew that they could be hidden. When I came back, I passed the toilet block and decided to look there. In the second cubicle in, I noticed there was this loose panel on the top and I thought that was new. I clambered up the side of the toilet and pushed it open and there were these two Red Cross parcels. I then knew we could catch this bloke when he came back to get them."

The toilets were located in the Number One Hut where the officers had their rooms. Lush attached a length of string on the door of the cubicle where the parcels were hidden.

> I ran it across the entrance and as you opened the door this string was up on top. We ran the string up in the air about eight or nine feet where no one would see it. We then punched a hole in the wall and took the string into John Paterson's office and at the end he tied his silver shaving mug. We blocked the doorway at one end of the toilets so that everyone had to go through the door at the other end and nobody would go up to the far end to use those cubicles where the parcels were hidden. The only bloke who could do that would be the one looking for the parcels.

The officers then maintained an all-night vigil. For two nights nothing happened but on the third night the trap was sprung when Paterson was awoken by the jangling shaving mug:

At about midnight, Paterson came out of his cubicle and said, 'Come on, we've got him!' We rushed into the toilet area and there is this little bloke standing in the cubicle looking up at the ceiling and it was clear someone had been up there. Paterson yelled, 'What are you doing here!' It frightened the hell out of me. We grabbed hold of this poor little bloke in a sort of friendly way and we said, 'What's going on?'

Percy Hunt was a private with the 2/19th Battalion from Stockton, New South Wales. Emaciated and desperately hungry, Hunt broke down and confessed that he had crept out late one night, broken the storeroom lock and stolen the two Red Cross parcels which he had hidden in the ceiling of the toilets. He told Lush and Paterson that he was deeply depressed over the deaths of four of his closest friends in the weeks beforehand: "All his mates had died, he thought he was going to be next and he wasn't going to die hungry. We were all in a weakened state, of course, but we were so upset when we saw his plight that we sent him back to his hut. I got up and picked the two parcels up and took them into my room."

The officers had no choice but to respond to the Japanese over the missing parcels but were determined as much as they could to avoid any repercussions, particularly for Private Hunt. The next night, after the work parade, Lush and Paterson went to see the senior Japanese guard on duty: "We told him we had found the culprit. 'Ah,' says the Jap, 'What do you plan to do with him?' Our reply was that we would punish him. We had discussed this beforehand and thought that if we gave him a couple of weeks of rest in the guard house we could double his food surreptitiously and the poor bugger might have a holiday and pick up a bit. So we said to the Jap, 'We will put him in the guard house for two weeks'. And he replied, 'One week!' So the bloke only got one week's rest in the guard house but it was at least a bit of a break from work."

The stolen parcels were duly handed back to the Japanese. After his week in the guardhouse, the officers continued to look out for Hunt's welfare. For a while they assigned him to light duties in the kitchen where his health began to improve. Percy Hunt would survive the war, serve with the fabled 3rd Battalion of the Royal Australian Regiment in Korea, return to his job as a roll mill operator with BHP and live to the venerable age of 93.

The withholding and regular theft of Red Cross parcels by the Japanese compounded the suffering of the prisoners and undoubtedly exacerbated the camp death toll. Lush and the other officers would plead with the guards to release more of the parcels, arguing that the men needed them so that they could work harder. They got short shrift: "The cruel part was that the Red Cross parcels had been forwarded to us in the camp and they were in the Quartermaster's Store. We knew they were there, yet the Japs were not prepared to hand them out to us. We were up against a brick wall. Nishikawa, the quartermaster, used to come down to our kitchen and get a couple of dixies full of rice that would have fed five or six men. He was also the one who stole the cocoa as well the Red Cross parcels."

Maintaining adequate clothing and footwear was a constant struggle. Most of the men had to make do with the clothing they had arrived in Japan with. Often it was not enough, especially during the severe winters, and as time wore on, clothes wore out. The men were lucky to have the services of a professional tailor to help them mend and maintain what little they had. Lance Sergeant Ken Cowell, an 8th Division signaller and Captain Paterson's batman, had worked as a tailor in Sydney before the war.

Cowell did a remarkable job. Men would leave shirts that were torn or unravelling and he would stitch them up and have them ready when the workers came back to the camp at night. The Japanese never supplied adequate clothing and the prisoners struggled to maintain appearances, not wanting to been seen dressed in rags as they marched through the main street of Kobe every day on their way to the shipyard. Lush had a towel made out of about a dozen pieces of worn out shirts. When anyone died there would be a raffle for their clothing.

The Japanese issued boots to the prisoners, but there were never enough and it was a constant struggle to persuade the guards to issue replacement pairs when they were needed. The prisoners frequently were ordered onto the parade ground for random boot inspections. The guards would walk along the lines of men and declare which ones were in urgent need of replacement boots which may or may not materialise. Paterson was forced to negotiate almost every day with Nishikawa for 20 or more pairs of boots and would receive just two or three pairs instead.

All the prisoners tried to have a spare pair of footwear and this would often involve improvisation. Bits and pieces of wood were found that could be shaped into sandals with a piece of strap cut from a haversack nailed on. And so a postwar Australian sartorial icon was born, according to Lush: "The local Japanese civilians had this type of sandal which was just a bit of wood with a bit of a strap across it and a nail on the wood to allow for a separation between the big toes. It was a very simple production and that developed in Australia years later as thongs. The Japs had these laid on for years before we came to Japan and that's how we saved our boots a bit when we had to wear them all the time."

By the new year of 1945, with the camp death toll rising and the health and morale of everyone in decline, many including Doug Lush began to doubt that the war would end in time to save them: "We were getting pretty low in health and I thought to myself at that stage that I wouldn't see the year out. We were all in such poor health and pretty low in spirits."

But their luck was about to change – dramatically.

Chapter 15

FIRE

We scorched and boiled and baked to death more people
in Tokyo that night of 9–10 March than went up
in vapour at Hiroshima and Nagasaki.

*General Curtis LeMay, commander of XXI Bomber Command,
US Air Force*[1]

By early 1945 the tide of the war was turning inexorably against
Japan. Nazi Germany's forces were being rolled back across Europe
towards their inevitable defeat, enabling the United States to focus
more heavily on the task of bringing Japan to heel. A series of victor-
ies in the Pacific between June and August 1944 had made that task
significantly easier.

During the Mariana Islands campaign, American forces captured
the Japanese-held islands of Guam, Saipan and Tinian. US Navy and
Air Force engineers immediately began work on the construction of
six airfields on the islands. The Americans had maintained sporadic air
bombing raids against strategic targets on the home islands of Japan
through 1943 and into 1944 but with limited success. The logistics of
flying bombers from India via forward bases in China had compromised
the effectiveness of Operation Matterhorn. But the Mariana Islands
were perfectly situated to mount an intensive air campaign against
Japan. As they lay about 1500 miles south of Tokyo, the American

B-29 Superfortress bombers could strike targets across most parts of the Japanese homeland and return without refuelling.

The advent of the new air bases also coincided with a dramatic change of tactics. As the Allies were doing with shocking effect in Europe, it was resolved to begin firebombing the major cities of Japan in the belief that this would demoralise the Japanese people and their leaders and hasten the end of the war. In November 1943 American air crews had begun testing a new type of incendiary weapon against a replica of a Japanese town built at the Dugway Proving Ground in Utah. The M69 bomb was armed with jellied petroleum: napalm. It would devastate the great cities of Japan – and their hapless residents – as brutally and comprehensively as did the firebombing of Germany by the Royal Air Force and its American ally.

By the war's end, the campaign driven by General Curtis LeMay's XXI Bomber Command would wreck 66 Japanese cities, kill more than 300,000 civilians and wound another million, raze more than 3.5 million homes and drive eight million people to shelter in the countryside. As historian Paul Ham wrote: "In the second half of 1945, LeMay's crews drew 100,000 tons of ordnance a month as they systematically burned Japan to a cinder."[2] The Allies were united in their resolve that this unprecedented assault on the civilian population of Japan was an unavoidable step to winning the war. Winston Churchill would famously tell the US Congress in a speech in May 1943: "Begin the process, so necessary and desirable, of laying the cities … of Japan in ashes, for in ashes they must surely lie before peace comes back to the world."

The first firebombing raid was launched against Tokyo on 9 March 1945. More than 300 Superfortress bombers – each loaded with 1520 incendiary bombs – took off from Saipan early in the evening. Shortly after midnight, air-raid sirens wailed as the waves of attacking aircraft swept low over the city and hundreds of thousands of civilians fled their houses of timber and paper in search of shelter from what they expected to be a conventional high-explosive bombing attack. Those in the immediate firing line had little hope of escape as, over the next three hours, almost half a million cylinders of napalm rained over some of the most densely-populated neighbourhoods on earth.

The bombs burst on impact, as Ham wrote, "spraying flaming jellied petroleum onto homes, attics, alleys, schools, hospitals, temples and factories. The high winds fanned these spot fires into a fireball that sucked in the surrounding oxygen. What followed was a fireball more terrible than anything seen in Germany."[3] An estimated 100,000 people perished and close to 400,000 homes were destroyed. Twelve US aircraft were lost. In the weeks that followed, firebombing raids were mounted against many other Japanese cities. After Tokyo, the worst affected were Nagoya, Yokohama, Kawasaki, Osaka – and Kobe.

The rain of fire reached the Kobe camp on 17 March 1945, St Patrick's Day, as Doug Lush recalled: "At eight o'clock that evening a B-29 appeared, circling, and it was lit up by searchlights. Obviously it was making a reconnaissance for what was to follow. About half an hour later, a number of B-29s appeared and commenced dropping incendiaries. There were large numbers of aircraft which flew in from various angles confusing the Japanese anti-aircraft guns and searchlights protecting both the city and the shipyards."

A total of 331 B-29s from all three wings of the XXI Bomber Command – the 73rd, 313th, and 314th bombardment wings – took part in the raid. Four key areas were targeted: the north-west corner of the city, the area south of the main rail line, the area north-west of the main rail station, and the area north-east of the third target.

In response, 280 Japanese fighters were scrambled. While only 96 of the fighters engaged the B-29s – and only three of the bombers were lost – this still constituted one of the biggest fighter responses seen by the Americans in a night raid over Japan.

Doug Lush and his fellow prisoners were stunned:

> They circled the entire area of Kobe dropping incendiaries and, of course, there was a lot of panic within our camp. Guards with fixed bayonets were positioned at various points and I was put in charge of Number Four hut with an armed guard who stood outside the entrance and wouldn't let me out. The other officers and prisoners in their huts were likewise locked up. When the bombs started falling, fires broke out all around the place. The incendiaries would split up into segments. There were octagonal steel casings and out of these casings would squirt heavy hot metal. As it fell on the ground it immediately ignited everything in its vicinity. Soon these casings were alight all around us.

John Paterson described the horrifying spectacle in his diary:

> Starting with one plane, the raid increased in intensity until they seemed to come from every direction – the whole sky was lit up and early in the piece a house 50 yards from us was hit and destroyed in a few minutes … This fire lit up the roofs of our huts until they showed out like the proverbial country 'dike' and I felt we'd be very lucky to escape. Our damage was one incendiary through the roof of the Dutch hut, one through the bathroom roof, and one at the kitchen door. They were all dealt with promptly, and beyond the holes in the roof, no damage. Houses right alongside the camp fences were destroyed, and I believe someone was killed nearby.[4]

Some of the officers and men had been released from the huts and ordered to form teams to help fight the fires raging around the camp. Ken Trumble had earlier been put in charge of the camp's fire brigade.

Trumble and his team, mostly members of the kitchen staff, were rushed outside the camp to help the terrified local residents. But most of the simple two-room cottages were already well alight. The best the prisoners could do was help the people drag out their bedding quilts and other belongings before their houses were engulfed by the inferno.

The prisoners were fortunate to have escaped the raid unharmed, and Paterson was not alone in wondering how much longer their luck would last: "All along I've believed this camp, situated as it is, is fairly safe, but now I think we'll be extremely lucky if we get through. Some prior warnings have been given out by the Yanks, I believe, as the raids on Osaka, Kobe, etcetera, have been expected – hence the military guards. The planes made a beautiful sight flying at about 8000 to 10,000 feet in full glare of searchlight – the prolific AA fire and a few fighters up apparently couldn't get near them. The doors could be seen opening to drop the bombs. What a peculiar feeling for one to see his own side in action."[5]

Doug Lush noted that the bombing had continued throughout the night until about 4am:

> A vast area of Kobe was destroyed – including the shipyards. It was a horrendous situation. The next morning we could see from where we were at the camp virtually all the way out to the shipyards. The whole area in between was destroyed. There were a lot of deaths. Some of the shops which adjoined the camp were constructed with light material such as bamboo and mud, with tiles stuck onto the external walls. After the firebombing all the tiles had dropped into the gutter. The bitumen on the little road outside the camp was molten and these tiles were floating down the river of bitumen.

Almost 9000 of Kobe's residents were later confirmed to have been killed in the firestorms, which destroyed an area of three square miles

– about 20 per cent of Kobe's urban area of 14 square miles. More than 650,000 homes were destroyed, and the homes of another million people were damaged. The brief interlude during which some of the prisoners were able to interact with local civilians as they battled the fires also gave them a glimpse of the struggle faced by ordinary Japanese as the American naval blockade – and the insatiable appetites of the Japanese war machine – drove the country to the edge of starvation.

Corporal Jack Nicholls, who had gone out with Ken Trumble's fire team, spoke to Doug Lush on his return: "Nicholls was talking to a Japanese doctor who told him how food was short, and he said that we were lucky to get any food at all because there was so little food available and a lot of people across Japan were suffering. So I think this starvation our camp was experiencing was at that stage pretty universal. They weren't getting food from anywhere else because all the sea lanes were now controlled by the Americans."

The day after the air attack, most of the fires had burnt themselves out. There was no power and water at the camp and teams had to be sent to cart water from a nearby well. The shocked Japanese guards lined up all the prisoners on the parade ground during the morning, but there were no recriminations. They singled out Ken Trumble and his fire team and spoke about the noble work that they had done in helping the neighbouring residents. Each man was given a packet of 10 cigarettes as a reward.

The destruction of the shipyard meant there was no more work for prisoners to do in Kobe. But a new chapter in their ordeal was about to begin. As they braced themselves for what might come next, Jack Chapman reflected on what they already had endured: "Our work in Kobe was now finished. We had been engaged in the construction of a number of oil tankers, perhaps seven or eight, and the yard's biggest ship, the *Taiho*, not that we were all that proud of this. During our time in this camp we had lost a total of 18 Australians; six Signals and 2/19 Battalion men in addition to several Dutch and Indonesians, all through mistreatment and illnesses caused by or accentuated by malnutrition. We had been prisoners of war for three years and three months, living on skeletal rations of rice and trying all the time to retain what hope and dignity we could."[6]

The men may not have known it at the time, but their reluctant contribution to the Japanese war effort had already been largely neutralised by the American navy. The 30,000-ton aircraft carrier *Taiho* – laid down at the Kawasaki shipyard in July 1941 and launched in April 1943 – had been lost a year before the shipyard was destroyed. She was felled by a torpedo from the American submarine USS *Albacore* during the Battle of the Philippines Sea, due, it was reported, to "explosions resulting from design flaws and poor damage control". A credit perhaps to the insolent workmanship of the Kobe POWs.

Chapter 16

IKUNO

After the Great Osaka Air Raid, there were no eyes
in which the progress of the war did not reflect the deep
hue of defeat. The Japanese public saw with their own eyes
the US Air Force bombers and reconnaissance planes flying
impressively throughout Japan. No matter how much
the military authorities were suppressing the truth,
it was clear that step-by-step our retreat was becoming
more inevitable, and danger was drawing nearer.

Kazuo Kobayashi, interpreter, Ikuno prisoner of war camp[1]

The destruction of the Kawasaki shipyard, and the devastation of the surrounding city, meant the days of the Kobe camp were numbered. With no work left for the prisoners and with the people of Kobe now locked in their own increasingly desperate struggle for survival, something had to give. The answer came quickly and, for most of the already severely debilitated men, it would mean renewed hardship in a more hostile and dangerous environment.

The Japanese resolved to split the Kobe prisoners into two parties. The enlisted men were to be sent to work in a coal mine near Fukuoka on the southern island of Kyushu; the officers were to relocate to a camp with other British and American officers at Ikuno, a small town in the hills of Hyogo prefecture about 100 miles north-west of Kobe.

John Paterson recorded the news in his diary:

> A bolt from the blue! I was called to the camp commander's office early this morning and informed that I, together with Lush, Trumble and [Dutch officer Lieutenant Hendrik Jan] Penning, leave at 5.30 tomorrow morning for an officers' camp. Nothing actually surprises me these days, but I didn't expect this, and have been thinking we'd maybe stay with the troops … Well, I just had to turn to and clean up everything, and try to pack my gear. I've accumulated a lot of stuff which has now to be discarded as I simply can't carry it. Records have to be handed over with money, etcetera (Camp Records including deaths to date were handed to Des Mulcahy). The camp commander thanked me for what I'd done, and the troops, after I announced the move, came in droves to say goodbye. My head was in a whirl all day as it's been such an uprooting after being settled for two and a half years.[2]

The officers' last night at the Kobe camp was disrupted by another air raid. They departed on schedule at 5.30am after a breakfast of chicken and some rice balls that they saved for their lunch. The commandant assigned several prisoners, including John Franklin, Norman Booth and Jack Nicholls, to take the camp truck to transport the officers' luggage, but Paterson and his colleagues had to walk the four miles to the main Kobe railway station. It was a stroll through a wasteland, as Paterson recorded in his diary:

> The bombed area has to be seen to be believed. Just as though an earthquake had levelled everything; a terrible sight. Left Kobe at 0730 and travelled south with curtains drawn, and consequently couldn't see anything. Changed trains and travelled in a less comfortable carriage to Ikuno … Marched one mile out along a deep valley alongside a beautiful stream. Here again our baggage was brought out by truck, which was a godsend. We passed a copper mine operated by Mitsubishi and reached the camp, which

consists of huts formerly occupied by mine employees ... We are now housed ten to a room. In mine are eight Australians and two Royal Scots – the balance consists of Americans and Englishmen – as far as I can see all good chaps ... I think it is going to be cold here in winter and very quiet away from everything.

The camp's official title was Osaka Number 4-B Ikuno. Paterson, Lush and Trumble were among the first arrivals after the Japanese resolved to gather officers from across the southern part of the country into one place. They soon were joined by several other Australians. Major Ronald Campbell was the Scots-born second in command of the legendary 2/40th Battalion, the nucleus of Sparrow Force which fought valiantly to defend Timor after the fall of Singapore. Tasmanian Lieutenant Brian Gordon had commanded one of the 2/40th mortar platoons. Like Campbell, Gordon had been mentioned in despatches for his bravery in action. South African–born Lieutenant Frank Pringle had enlisted in Sydney and served with the 2/3 Motor Ambulance Convoy. Lieutenant Keith Goddard was with the Australian Army Service Corps unit attached to the 22nd Brigade. Initially, the Australians shared the camp with 43 British and American officers, including one who became their leader. Lieutenant Colonel Franklin Morris Fliniau was an infantry officer captured at Iloilo City on the Philippines island of Panay when it fell to the Japanese in April 1942.

Before the Australians could move into their new quarters they had to deal with the mess left behind by the Korean workers who had been camped there before their arrival. It was a task that incensed Doug Lush: "These huts were lousy. The Koreans had done their 'business' on the floors and there were bugs crawling around everywhere. It was filthy, so we had to organise buckets of hot water and it took us many hours to finally fix it all up and make it inhabitable. The stench was shocking. I'll never forget it! We eventually settled down after cleaning it all up."

Soon after the Australians had settled in, the camp's numbers were swelled with the arrival of about 400 British prisoners who had been working at the Sumitomo steelworks at Wakayama near Osaka. The British enlisted men were sent to work at the nearby copper and silver mine. The rich deposits in the area had been mined since the 8th century. Eventually, the officers were sent out in work gangs to the surrounding hills, as Lush recalled:

> They didn't know what to do with us in the first days. Finally, they marched us off from the back of the camp up into the hills. There was an area there with a running stream and a hillside like Belgrave [in Victoria's Dandenong Ranges]. There was bracken and so forth and rocks and the Japanese said we had to clear it all. Dotted around the place were these dwarf sheoak trees which we had to remove. The Japs insisted that we pick up the large rocks and build a wall with them, and put the soil back behind the rocks and plant sweet potatoes. Of course, they grow pretty quick these sweet potatoes and the Japs got onto them and pinched them. After that we cut the tubas off and kept them covered by soil so when they took off with them there was no potato attached to the top.

Lush, along with Paterson, Trumble and a Scots officer, Lieutenant Douglas Baird, were assigned to operate the machinery used to clear the sheoaks and pull out their stumps by wrapping chains around the roots. In charge of the gangs clearing the dwarf sheoaks was an American officer, Captain Oel Johnson, assisted by Lieutenant Bob Broadwater – both of whom had worked for Coca Cola and would become senior executives of the company after the war. From April 1945, Johnson and Broadwater would share a hut with the Australian officers, John Paterson declaring them to be "good, sensible chaps". Johnson would become a firm friend of Doug Lush.

Born in Alabama, the 35-year-old Johnson had been working in Manila, running production for Coca Cola's Far Eastern Division, when the war broke out. Called up for military service in December 1941, four months later he was commanding an artillery unit when Bataan fell. He was then forced to join the infamous 'Death March' during which more than 6000 American and Filipino troops died, as he would recount: "As for my part of the march out of Bataan, it was about 50 miles, 30 of which was made in one continuous march. I was in the first group; most of the atrocities occurred in the rear groups. Many men were falling out of my group as many of them had malaria, dysentery and sunstroke. I saw men beaten and stabbed with bayonets because they could not continue."[3]

Johnson would see many more die of disease, starvation and brutality over the following months at the infamous Camp O'Donnell in Tarlac, in the Central Luzon region of the Philippines: "Soon after our arrival, the death rate mounted as dysentery, malaria, yellow jaundice and other diseases raged through the camp ... There was practically no medicine. The American authorities asked for medicine as many men were sick and dying. They were told by the Japanese that they were not interested in the number of sick, but the number of dead, in order to keep the records straight."

Despite suffering debilitating illness himself, including a severe case of dysentery, Johnson survived O'Donnell and other equally grim camps in the Philippines before being shipped to Japan with another 1500 American prisoners in November 1942 – in conditions as arduous as those suffered by the Australians of C Force several weeks later. He was assigned to a camp at Tanagawa on Honshu Island, where the prisoners worked to build a breakwater for a dry dock and submarine base, before his eventual transfer to Ikuno.

At their new camp, the Americans and British became resourceful at augmenting the meagre camp rations. Some English prisoners got hold of guinea pigs which they started breeding. The Americans would search the hills for non-venomous snakes that they would skin, chop into smaller pieces and boil. Others would collect small bracken ferns to eat, to the detriment of the health of many of the prisoners, including Lush: "With the snakes and some ferns it became a chicken soup, to go with our rice, and we lived on this for about five months or so, every day. On my return to Australia, it was discovered that due to this bracken fern diet I had received toxic poisoning to the liver, which the doctors at first thought was caused by over indulging in alcohol. The effects of this lasted some years after the war."

When they were not working, the men developed a passion for card games, and the Australians were not averse to a little cheating against their British and American opponents, as Lush confessed: "On our days off, we used to play cards: Culbertson's Bridge. Culbertson developed the pattern which we used to play Bridge (Contract Bridge). Trumble and I used to do some terrible things. We used to cough to indicate whether we had a good hand or not. We played for cigarettes."

During the months at Ikuno the officers' spirits were raised when the Japanese announced that they would be allowed to send more messages to their families back in Australia. One day Lush and several others were called out during the daily parade and told they could prepare a message: "I said, 'I'm in Japan, I'm in Osaka, I'm in pretty good health and things are going fairly well'. The messages were recorded but I rather doubt that they were ever played. It was probably all showmanship. My family had first heard in May 1944 through Government correspondence that I was a POW. They said that I had been reported to be in a POW camp. After the war my mother said she never received any letter or photograph of me whilst I was a prisoner of war."

Regular bashings continued to be part of life in the camp, but less so and with less severity than at Kobe. The officers enjoyed cordial relationships with a number of the guards and civilian employees, particularly a young interpreter named Kazuo Kobayashi and Sergeant Major Yoshinari Minemoto, who headed the camp administration.

Kobayashi was a pacifist conscripted to the war effort despite his best efforts to have no part of it. As a high school student in Kobe's Hyogo prefecture, he had fallen in love with the English language under the guidance of an American teacher named Roy Smith. When the war began, Kobayashi and his student friends resisted the propaganda of denouncing Westerners as 'foreign devils' – and the pressure to shun any use of the English language: "We would go to nearby coffee shops and chat with each other in English, building up our conversational abilities. Even while walking down the street, we'd speak in English. The townsfolk certainly thought it was strange that we pacifists used the enemy's language on purpose to agitate against the war. 'America and Britain are enemies! It's absurd to use English,' one gentleman lectured us angrily. One lady, the leader of the Women's Patriotic Society, quietly warned us with a stiff reminder, 'You'd better stop using English or the military police will come after you'."[4]

Kobayashi initially had avoided being conscripted into the army because of his poor physical condition but in March 1944 he was approached by a revered teacher from his middle-school days with an offer he could not refuse. Mr Toijiro Kuranishi was now Lieutenant Kuranishi, commandant of the Tanagawa POW camp – where the American officers at Ikuno were first held. Kuranishi needed a camp interpreter and insisted that Kobayashi was the man for the job: "If young people do not find employment to be of service to the country in some indirect way, they will not be able to recover their minds and bodies."[5]

Kobayashi accepted the job at Tanagawa where he soon established a rapport with the American officers, including Oel Johnson, Bob Broadwater and Frank Fliniau, who introduced him to the American vernacular. Soon the 21-year-old interpreter was interceding with Lieutenant Kuranishi to moderate the violent behaviour of some of the guards and to smooth conflicts and misunderstandings. And soon Kobayashi – nicknamed 'Fireball' by the prisoners – and his friend Sergeant Minemoto were teaching Japanese to the Americans. The young interpreter's concern for the prisoners would extend to buying medicines with his own money and smuggling them into the camp. When the Americans were transferred to Ikuno in March 1945, Kobayashi went with them.

Kobayashi saw himself differently to his fellow Japanese in the camps:

> As an interpreter, I was not simply a language intermediary but I was understanding in some way the psychology of it all and, without breaking any military rules, feeling acutely that I should become to these men 'one who understands languages and psychology' to dispel their fears, and in the midst of their privation, to make them breathe, if only a little, the air of freedom … life at Ikuno enabled me to have a genial interaction with the POWs. As the days went by, my sister's two sons would occasionally stop by the camp and the men would carry the boys around on their shoulders, a picture of playful innocence.[6]

After the horrors of firebombing in Kobe, life at the Ikuno camp was relatively tranquil: there were no bombing raids. But the officers' good fortune was not shared by the men they left behind at Kobe.

Chapter 17

YOSHI

We weren't too keen on life at Kobe but we soon realised
that we were to be much worse off in the coalmine
called Camp 26.

Lloyd Ellerman[1]

Life for the men assigned to the Kawasaki shipyard had been a constant struggle against hunger, illness and abuse during their two and a
half years imprisoned at Kobe. But worse was to follow. In early May
1945 most of the Australians left behind at Kobe by their officers were
transferred to Kyushu, the south-westernmost of Japan's main islands.
Their destination was the Yoshikuma coalmine in Fukuoka prefecture.

The old 'Yoshi' mine had been closed for many years as it was considered too dangerous to operate but had reopened in 1939 with the
deployment of Korean forced labourers, who were starved, paid little
or no wages and died in large numbers. Now it was the turn of the
Allied prisoners of war – 197 Australians, 101 British and two Dutch.

The workers were billeted in vermin-infested huts in what was
officially known as Fukuoka Number 26-B Keisen Camp. The camp
was encircled by three-yard-high electrified fences and patrolled by
brutal guards. The mine was a death trap. Bob Chapman shakes his
head at the memory, more than 70 years on: "It was an old mine. As

153

you went along to get to the coalface the roof was propped up with timber planks at the side and on top and all the way along they were sagging under the weight above. We could hear the roof falling 50 yards away. Many times there were cave-ins near where we were working. We were lucky not to be killed. That was the worst thing I have ever done in my life."[2]

The miners worked day and night shifts of up to 14 hours and it took them an hour to reach the coalface – which was about a mile underground – and an hour to return. The conditions were treacherous, as Charlie 'Slim' Bone, a signaller from Geelong in Victoria, recalled: "We had blokes from NSW who had worked in coalmines and they said that in Australia the miners' union would not work a coalface under six feet. We were working 18 inches, lying on our bellies with hooks scraping the coal out. They were in such a bad way for coal."[3]

The Yoshikuma mine was and still is owned by the Aso family, one of Japan's most powerful dynasties. For more than 60 years after the war, the company denied Allied prisoners had been used as slave labour at the mine. When the *New York Times* reported on the mine's shameful history in 2007, the Japanese Foreign Ministry issued an extraordinary statement that declared: "Our Government has not received any information the company has used forced labourers. It is totally unreasonable to make this kind of judgemental description without presenting any evidence."

It was no coincidence that at the time that statement was released, the Foreign Minister of Japan was Taro Aso, a former president of the family company who would a year later become Prime Minister of Japan. The lies of the Aso Mining Company – which were finally abandoned in 2008 in the face of international outrage – were an insult not only to the men who suffered as slave labourers but also to the memory of the two Australian POWs whose deaths were indelible evidence of the truth: Leslie Wilkie and John Watson. The miracle was that many more did not perish.

Wilkie, a 28-year-old private with the Australian Army Ordnance Corps from Gladstone, Queensland, suffered from beri-beri and acute pneumonia and died on 11 June 1945.

John Watson, a 32-year-old signalman from Brighton-le-Sands in New South Wales, succumbed to the effects of acute bronchitis, malnutrition and dysentery on 19 July.

Mick Kildey nursed Watson during his final hours: "He was just a skeleton and I will always remember him whimpering with pain when I just accidentally bumped his backside, because it was just skin and bone."[4]

Kildey recounted how all of the prisoners were starved and beaten "half to death" while forced to toil underground over very long hours, seven days a week, with no rest days: "When the shifts changed we couldn't sleep for 24 hours and food and clothing were never enough. We were rags and bones. Yet we were sent down to the Number 16 level – really dangerous – and two levels below where any Japanese would go. There were cave-ins all the time."[5]

Athol Hill, a private with the 2/19th Battalion, predicted that the death toll at Yoshikuma would have soared if the war had continued into the northern winter of 1945. He gave a statement about conditions at the camp to investigators when he arrived in Manila in October, on his way home to Australia:

> Food was very poor – the worst we ever received. The men were going down in health through malnutrition and starvation. If the war had not ended there were many of us who would not have seen another three months out. We worked down the coal mine

up to 14 hours a day – it was an old mine that had been opened up. It was falling in everywhere. Dozens of men here hit. There was water down the mine. The air was foul. Sick men there were forced to work as usual. There was a lot of disease there, mostly malnutrition and dysentery ... Medical supplies were nil ... They were actually gradually killing us through work. A few months back we all felt we would never see the next winter through.[6]

After several months enduring the appalling conditions at the mine, and the endless demands for more and more coal to be extracted, the exhausted miners decided to go on strike. In the thick of the brazen, and potentially deadly, rebellion was Lloyd Ellerman:

We decided down the mine that we'd had enough. So we were very impolite to the Jap miners and went on strike over their demands for more and more skips. So we stopped work. It seemed that we prisoners agreed on this action with one voice. We walked out of the mine in the usual way except that the civilian 'minders' were bringing up the rear. We talked about what might be in store for us when we reached the surface and met the armed guards, but we had no second thoughts on the way up. To our surprise, nothing was said of our action. Obviously, the civilian guards were more afraid of the repercussions than we were. That fixed the matter of more and more skips, and output needs were therefore stabilised. I doubt if this kind of action was repeated anywhere else.[7]

The prospect of a further confrontation between the captives and the captors that might not have ended as peacefully was averted days later when the war in the skies over Japan took a cataclysmic new turn, as Ellerman recalled: "The next thing was seeing a huge white cloud over the mountains in the direction of Nagasaki on 9th August 1945. We gathered from Korean guards that there had been a huge raid but we knew no more for some time. It was, of course, the second atom bomb."[8]

Des Mulcahy had just returned from night shift in the mine and was preparing to sleep for the day: "We heard this terrific boom. I walked out and looked in the sky and we could see this terrific cloud rising up. I didn't think much of it. I thought, 'That must have been a terrible big ammunition dump they hit down there. Look at the size of it. It's enormous.' I went back to bed again and it wasn't for about three days until I realised that it was an atom bomb."[9]

Chapter 18

LIBERATION

The source from which the sun draws its powers
has been loosed against those who brought war
to the Far East.

Statement by President Harry Truman, 6 August 1945[1]

In August 1939, as German troops prepared to invade Poland and trigger World War II, Albert Einstein wrote a prophetic letter to US President Franklin D. Roosevelt in collaboration with the Hungarian-born physicist Leo Szilard. "It appears almost certain," the letter intoned, that "a nuclear chain reaction in a large mass of uranium … could be achieved in the immediate future." Einstein went on to warn that "extremely powerful new bombs of a new type may thus be constructed" that could be used to devastating effect.

By the end of the 1930s, a series of discoveries by scientists in Denmark, Britain, Germany and France had led to the crucial finding that fission in a uranium nucleus liberates the two or three neutrons necessary to sustain a chain reaction. Roosevelt responded immediately to Einstein's clarion call and established, in great secrecy, the massive scientific and military corporation that would ensure the United States was the first nation to build an atomic bomb. The Manhattan Project achieved its objective on 16 July 1945 at Alamogordo Air Base in the deserts of New Mexico. At 5.29am a flash "like a giant magnesium flare" erupted and the surrounding hills were "bathed in a brilliant light, as if someone had turned the sun on with a switch".[2]

In the early hours of 6 August 1945 an American Superfortress bomber fired its four engines and began to taxi towards the runway at the United States Air Force base on Tinian Island in the Northern Marianas. A newly painted title on the forward fuselage read 'Enola Gay', the name of the mother of the captain, Lieutenant Colonel Paul Tibbets. In the hold sat 'Little Boy', the code name for the 4400 kilogram bomb which carried a blast yield equivalent to 15 kilotons of TNT: the world's first atomic weapon.

The crew were unaware of their cargo and the mission until their pre-flight briefing when Captain William 'Deak' Parsons, who would arm the bomb during the flight, told them: "It is the most destructive weapon ever produced ... the loudest, the brightest, the hottest thing ... since Creation."[3] Even after take-off, the crew did not know their final destination. Tokyo was a 12-hour round trip away, via Iwo Jima. As they approached the Japanese mainland, the target was confirmed. It would be the northern city of Hiroshima.

At 8.14am local time, the target – the Aioi Bridge in the centre of the city – appeared in the bombardier's sites. A minute later the bomb bay doors opened and the aircraft lurched violently upwards from the sudden loss of weight as the giant bomb nose-dived towards the unsuspecting population of 350,000 people beginning their day below. An intense burst of light was followed by a rippling wave of heat travelling at 7200 miles per hour that tossed the plane about like a toy. A fiery sea of what looked like lava covered the whole city and spread up into the foothills. "Down below all you could see was a black boiling nest," Tibbets said later. "I didn't think about what was going on down on the ground ... I didn't order the bomb to be dropped, but I had a mission to do."[4]

News of the terrifying new power in America's hands spread rapidly around the world but slowly in Japan. The devastation of Hiroshima – where 78,000 had perished and another 37,000 were wounded on the day – was so pervasive that crippled communications slowed the reporting of the impact to Tokyo and the rest of the country. When word did come through, the military leadership, inured by months of huge casualties from the American firebombing campaign and generally indifferent to the suffering of the civilian population, thought initially that they were dealing merely with another, albeit particularly ferocious, bombing. The magnitude of what they were facing was finally dawning when the second atomic bomb was unleashed on Nagasaki three days later.

At Ikuno, 200 miles to the west of Hiroshima, Doug Lush and his fellow prisoners were unaware of the apocalyptic event unfolding on the other side of the island of Honshu. In his brief diary entry for 6 August, John Paterson noted that he had counted 17 waves of bombers passing overhead the previous night: "A very big force which, it is believed, did Kobe over."[5] But there was nothing about the single aircraft that had devastated another city more comprehensively than the hundreds of other aircraft that had been relentlessly firebombing Japan's biggest cities for weeks on end.

When 'Fat Man' – a bigger and more deadly bomb – was dropped on Nagasaki three days after the Hiroshima attack, 24 Australian POWs were just 1850 yards from ground zero. They were at the infamous Fukuoka Number 14 camp where they worked in the steelworks and coal mines of the Mitsubishi Heavy Industry Company. Hurled to the ground by the force of the blast and buried in the wreckage of buildings, they sustained minor injuries but miraculously none of them was killed.

The 8th Division signallers toiling at the Yoshikuma coal mine near the city of Fukuoka, about 100 miles south of Nagasaki, were stunned by the distant spectacle. South Australian Signalman Arthur Gigger had just come off night shift in the mine on the morning of 9 August: "I was trying to get to sleep but I heard the air raid siren and then I heard a whopper of a bang in the distance. I didn't take much notice and then someone yelled out, 'Come and look at this!' We all went outside and here was this great big mushroom cloud in the distance. We later found out that it was the atomic bomb."[6]

When news of the blasts reached Ikuno, the Japanese played down their impact, as Doug Lush recounted: "They might have been frightened but they didn't show it. They just said quietly that a bomb had been dropped and about two hundred thousand people were killed and there had been a lot of destruction. We didn't know it was an atomic bomb at that stage, but we knew it must have been a big bomb, so we continued to work in the normal way. Then the second bomb was dropped on Nagasaki, by which time of course things were getting tense."

August 14 was the fourth anniversary of John Paterson's arrival in Malaya. But there was nothing to celebrate. A promised handout of Red Cross parcels did not eventuate: "Hungry all day, not even a cup of tea now," he wrote in his diary. Two days later, the news arrived that the prisoners had long awaited: "This morning after a siren-free night we were lucky to hear through two useful avenues that the Emperor had called off the war after a day of prayer ... Nothing has come yet from the Nips, except that there is no work for anybody ... The interpreter has indicated that it is so, but that certain people in the country do not agree with the Emperor! Needless to say, we are right up in the air.

My personal feelings are of uncertainty and I can't get really excited. Maybe that will come later when an official announcement is made."[7]

Ken Trumble captured the tense anticipation in his diary: "Is it possible? After three and a half years of anxious waiting, blighted hopes, blind ducks and like disappointments, has our salvation come at last? Everybody self-consciously happy, but no outright jubilation as yet. Still, haven't we always said, three months after Germany? We vacillate, we sit down and get up again and walk about aimlessly. We play poker (I lose), the feeling that it is over increases with the day."[8]

Confirmation came a week later when Lieutenant Colonel Fliniau and the senior British officer, Major Alfred Houghton, were called in by the camp commandant, First Lieutenant Hideo Naruwa, known among his charges as 'The Coolie'. They were advised that an armistice would be signed on the 30th and, while the men were still officially prisoners until that time, full control of the camp was now being handed over to them. In a personal act of surrender, Naruwa handed his sword to Fliniau and declared: "In accordance with the surrender of the Japanese military, I hereby transfer authority to you."[9] It was a particularly poignant moment for Fliniau who, three years earlier, had been required to organise the American surrender to Japanese forces on the Philippines island of Panay where he had been chief of staff to the US area commander, Colonel Albert Christie.

Paterson was briefed immediately about the extraordinary moment by his US and British colleagues: "So now we are officially informed that we are the victors – something that I was afraid would not happen until we marched out ... He said that we should still salute NCOs etc., but I am afraid that I have given my last salute to a Nip."[10]

The wave of relief that swept the camp with the confirmation that their liberation was imminent would be tempered by a sharpened fear that the Japanese might still respond to their defeat with deadly reprisals against their prisoners, as Doug Lush recalled:

> We were mindful of the fanatical attitude of the Japanese and we had a suspicion that they could have begun killing all the POWs. And had the Allies invaded Japan that certainly would have happened, there's no question about that. In our particular case, we thought they might herd us all into the administrative block and set fire to it – a very simple way of getting rid of us all. We knew what they were capable of when they were mad, like they did after the Battle of Muar when they tied up all the prisoners – burn them, cover them up and leave no trace.

Some of the British officers suspected that tunnels within the mine were being prepared and that prisoners would be herded into them and then blown up. Lush and Trumble discussed the possibility of escaping when they were away from the camp with a work party: "We thought we could get out of the camp and go out to where we were working clearing land as we knew the area pretty well, and we believed that we could have hung out for two or three weeks as there was running water. In the end, it didn't come to this as the Japs were told to put down their arms and surrender by their Emperor."

Harold Dwyer, a signaller from Albury in NSW, was told by a Japanese officer that there were plans to exterminate all of the prisoners at the Yoshikuma mine: "This animal conveyed the startling information that camp inmates at Yoshi were to be herded into one of the extinct coal mines in a hill face near the camp on 18 August (three days after capitulation), the entrance sealed off and drums of petrol poured through ventilators and set alight. There was no reason whatsoever to doubt or discount this information."[11]

More tangible evidence of the potential risk that all prisoners would be exterminated was discovered at another of the camps in the Nagasaki area. According to Mick Kildey, an 'Extermination Order' dated 14 August 1945 – the day before the war ended – was found in the camp safe after the Japanese guards departed. The order directed the guards: "When you take refuge from bomb explosions you must make every prisoner being in one spot under strict caution and kill them all."[12]

Lloyd Ellerman was convinced that the atomic bombs saved not only his life and the lives of his fellow prisoners but also countless other civilians and combatants:

> Evidence abounds that the Japanese intended to liquidate all POWs in Japan in the event of an American landing on the main Japanese islands. In many camps, caves and ditches had been prepared. We were all at extreme risk at the time the two atom bombs were dropped. They clearly saved our lives. Needless to say, we do not readily take the view that the US should not have dropped the bombs. People also forget, or do not appreciate, the devastation and loss of life which resulted from the big raids with conventional bombs. Had a landing been needed to end the war, it is no great exaggeration to say that another half a million people would have died – mostly Japanese.[13]

At Ikuno, and at many other camps, the prisoners were instructed to paint the letters "PW" in bold yellow on the roofs of their huts to indicate to the American flight crews that it was a POW camp. Soon after 3pm on August 28 the men were stirred by noise of an approaching aircraft, as Doug Lush recounted: "We all rushed out and shortly afterwards a B29 shot through the clouds about 1500 feet up followed, after 10 minutes or so, by another. They both missed the camp but came back again. We waved and yelled like mad and then one saw us, banked sharply and rolled. It gave us a marvellous thrill. After a minute or two it came right over the camp at about 800 feet and we could read 'PW Supplies' on the wings. Out came bundles of pamphlets which fluttered down all around the valley and hills."

The men scrambled out from the camp to gather up the pamphlets. Written in English and Dutch and headlined "ALLIED PRISONERS", they declared: "The Japanese Government has surrendered. You will be evacuated by Allied nations forces as soon as possible. Until that time, your present supplies will be augmented by air-drop of US food, clothing and medicines. The first drop of these items will arrive within one (1) or two (2) hours." After detailing the American manna that would shortly rain from the heavens, there was a warning typed in bold capital letters: "DO NOT OVEREAT OR OVERMEDICATE." It was a warning that would soon be completely ignored.

Not long after the pamphlets had been dropped, more planes flew over and 44-gallon drums rained from the sky laden with clothing and food – tins of soup, chocolate, Spam and – to the consternation of men who had eaten little else for more than three years – rice. Ken Trumble was ecstatic: "Oh boy! What a treat for the kids! Better than Xmas. The Nips knocked cockeyed speechless by this display. After three and a half years of squalor, the ordinary G.I. stuff dropped is sheer luxury."[14]

The officers were forced to step in to try to control the situation as men rushed out of the camp and into the hills, breaking open the barrels that had not already broken open and gorging themselves on the largesse. While the reaction of starving men was understandable, it was essential to organise an orderly and equitable distribution of the food, especially to ensure that the sick got their share.

A system of distribution for the food and vitamin supplements was quickly established. More drops followed with additional food and clothing, including shirts, trousers and boots – a godsend for men who had been reduced to living in rags, as Lush recounted:

> Everyone got a clean shirt and a pair of slacks and we all turned out looking pretty clean after what we had been living with. That was when these size nine boots floated down. I saw these boots that had hooked themselves high in one of the electrical lines that ran into the camp. I just had to get those boots. I don't know how but I got up there and got them. They were a size too big for me but they fitted as far as I was concerned and I wore them from then on. In fact, I kept them with me and brought them home with me. I kept using those boots for ten years after the war. They were split-hide – beautiful American boots.

While they waited impatiently for formal confirmation of what would happen next, the prisoners began to roam beyond the gates. On his first outing as a relatively free man, Doug Lush stumbled upon an officer of the Kenpeitai, the infamous Japanese military police. The officer was summarily relieved of his sword and pistol – both of which would travel home to Australia as prized mementos of that special day.

At the Yoshikuma camp, the newly-liberated Australian prisoners were relieving their former captors of other treasures. One day they intercepted two Japanese corporals in an army truck carrying a dressed bullock of about 150 kilograms. Warrant Officer Des Mulcahy had the truck and its precious cargo diverted immediately to the camp kitchen where the fires were stoked and the beast butchered – before the hapless corporals were ordered back to their base on foot. It would not be the last word, as Mulcahy recounted:

> We could smell the meat cooking and the boys were all walk-
> ing around with their noses in the air with this beef. We hadn't
> had beef for two years. Another runner came down and he said,
> 'Quick, come up, there is a carload of senior Jap officers up there

and they want to see you.' I walked up. I could see they were pretty senior men so, as I went past the guardhouse I said to the sergeant, 'Have four of your men out there with rifles standing ready, something might develop here.' I went on out. I saluted this bloke – he was a full colonel – and he saluted me back. He spoke good English. He said, 'Excuse me sir, but you have con-fiscated the week's ration supply for my thousand odd troops. They will not have any meat at all this week and they will be very disgruntled.' I said, 'That's bad luck. I have 200 men here who haven't seen meat for two years. They have been disgruntled for two years and I have had to put up with it. I would advise you to get in your car and go home and leave the meat here. If you put on a song and dance I will confiscate your car and you and your officers and friends can walk home' ... He blinked his eyes a few times and looked around and saw I meant it – he saw the four blokes lined up there with rifles – so he saluted and got in the car and went away. I never saw a sign of them afterwards.[15]

As they explored the district surrounding their camps, the Australians saw in stark detail the desperate poverty in which many Japanese civilians were surviving. Des Mulcahy was one of many deeply affected by what he saw:

They had been through a terrible time, the Japanese civilians. They had been on a meagre ration which would be enough for them to live on, that's all, and they were completely controlled by the army and had to do what the army told them. When we walked past them, they used to break down and cry ... If they had done that during the war they would have been bashed by the Japanese [soldiers] ... The poor old women who walked by would wipe their eyes and sort of nod their head in shame ... We were sympathetic to them, very sympathetic to them. We were free and they still weren't free. They were still under the control of the army. At that stage, they didn't know what the future held for them.[16]

Soon after the first air drops of relief supplies at Ikuno, John Paterson wandered into the village closest to the camp. He was amazed at how servile the Japanese had become, with adults "bowing and scraping" while "kids everywhere" begged for chewing gum. On 30 August he explored even further afield: "This morning went for an eight-mile walk with Oel Johnson, Lush and Trumble – through the village and out to the valley beyond. Wandered through villages and farms, saw … lots of children who treated us like the 'Pied Pier'. On the way back, called in at the Air Corps Meteorological Station and talked pidgin English to the staff with three very shy girl clerks in the background. I like the little girls, dear little kids who won't get much out of this world, I am afraid."[17]

On their return to the camp they were disappointed to learn that a delegation of officers sent to the nearby city of Himeji to meet with Red Cross representatives had returned without any definite news about their departure. The following afternoon 'Bonnie Leslie' arrived with orders for 13 American officers, including Oel Johnson, to move to other camps. While Paterson, Lush and Trumble waited, they filled their time harvesting and eating the produce from hillside gardens and playing poker.

At 1pm on 2 September, the entire camp was called onto the parade ground. John Paterson recorded a moment that all of the prisoners had longed for throughout their years of imprisonment: "The Coolie [Lieutenant Naruwa] spoke in Nip followed by Houghton's translation which stated that the Armistice had been signed this morning at 0900 on the USS *Missouri*, the largest battleship. So we are FREE at last. He handed the camp over to Major Pitt and hoped it would be without incident and that we would return safely to our homes.

Houghton then proposed that we should thank the Coolie, if you please. He was the only one to do so, however."[18]

By 3pm there had still not been a broadcast in English of the Armistice terms so the men resolved to hold their own flag-raising parade, as Paterson recorded: "All the troops lined up on the road opposite the camp with officers in the front. Padre McNeil read our prayer which was followed by the breaking of the Union Jack then the salute, three cheers and the singing of the National Anthem. A really impressive parade ... Rain poured down, unfortunately, and the homemade flag (taken from Nip eiderdowns, a white sheet dyed blue) inclined to play up a bit. However, it was a grand sight never to be forgotten."

The following day a truck carrying more relief supplies arrived from Osaka with the first news of the nuclear strikes. "Newspapers refer to atom bombs dropped on Hiroshima and Nagasaki with terrible effect," Paterson wrote in his diary. "I'm afraid some of our people might have suffered. They say something about 90,000 killed and 180,000 casualties."

The final reckoning of the toll on its own people from Japan's reckless military adventurism would be staggering. Between January 1944 and August 1945, the United States dropped 157,000 tons of bombs on Japanese cities. The US Strategic Bombing Survey estimated that 333,000 people were killed, including 80,000 in the attack on Hiroshima and 40,000 in the Nagasaki attack. Other estimates put the toll much higher. Fifteen million of Japan's population of 72 million were left homeless.

Chapter 19

OSAKA

Fellow citizens, the war is over ...
At this moment let us offer thanks to God.
Let us remember those whose lives were given
that we may enjoy this glorious moment and may
look forward to a peace which they have won for us.

Australian Prime Minister Ben Chifley
announcing the war's end, 15 August 1945

The Australians were now free men and their former captors quickly sought to make amends for the suffering they had inflicted – or at least to soften the coming judgment of their actions by Japan's new American masters. On the night of 4 August 1945 all the officers were invited to a 'sukiyaki' party at the home of the president of the Mitsubishi mine company.

After sharing some cigarettes, the guests were directed downstairs to where two big rooms had been opened into one and ushered to low square tables with charcoal braziers set in the middle. On each table was a brass pan filled with chopped beef and onions stewing in soy sauce and sugar. Alongside was a tantalising array of other dishes, including salmon and mixed fish. As soon as the men were seated, young women dressed in beautiful kimonos with elaborately styled hair appeared to serve sake. After a speech from Mr Tomita, the managing director, in which declared that the company had done its best for the prisoners and regretted their past hardships, everyone dived into the sukiyaki. It was the best food they had eaten for three years.[1]

During the party, which lasted four and half hours, the girls danced and a few people sang and American music was played on a gramophone. On leaving, each of the men was presented with a small china bowl. John Paterson relished the transformation in his captors: "From conversations, I gathered the impression that they have taken the count good and proper and accepted our superiority as a matter of course. The arrogant attitude has gone completely and everything now depends on what 'Marshal MacArthur' decides to do, etc."[2]

The following night there were more festivities when Paterson, Doug Lush and several other officers were invited to another dinner at the home of Mr Nakamura, the mine vice-president. At the end of another lavish meal accompanied by large quantities of beer and whiskey, the men were each presented with a fan, a silk handkerchief and a small novelty booklet. The next morning, now well fed and clothed, the Australians decided it was time to leave, as Doug Lush recalled: "Captain Paterson came to me and said, 'Get a dixie full of rice. We are going'. There was now no obligation for us to stay there and it was only that we were friends with some of the other officers that we had not gone sooner. And as soon as we left I believe so did some of the others."

At 7.30 on the morning of 6 September, Lush and Paterson set off for Kyoto. They travelled by train via Wadayama and Fukuchiyama. At Wadayama, the entire railway staff stood at attention for them on the station platform, brought tea, produced an escort and organised good seats on the next train to Kyoto. As Lush recounted: "There was a Kenpeitai, one of the military police, with a sword and a [Luger pistol] at his side. I said to my friend, 'Make him salute.' Paterson gave the order and he did it ... it was an incredible feeling."[3] The pair reached Kyoto at 3pm.

Paterson was shocked by the state of the fabled city which had not been bombed but was dirty and dilapidated with thousands of people sleeping in the streets and in and around the railway station. After being turned away at two hotels, they found a room at one close to the station – "a big, modern, filthy unserviced place with no water laid on and little else". After a simple meal of fish soup, rice and fish rissoles, Paterson recorded having "an interesting experience at a cost of Y250" – an experience, perhaps, that sated long-repressed appetites of another kind.

Early the next morning, Paterson and Lush headed for Osaka, a 45-minute journey by electric train. They found the city in ruins from the relentless American bombing. Their destination was the Red Cross hospital that had been established in a disused sports stadium. They were welcomed by Surgeon Lieutenant Commander John Page. Page had joined the Royal Navy in 1930 after studying medicine at Trinity College, Dublin. Appointed to the Royal Naval Hospital in Hong Kong in 1939, he had been taken prisoner in December 1941 and later sent to Japan. Page would later give evidence describing the Osaka hospital as a "death hole" where Japanese doctors had performed cruel experimental operations on seven or eight prisoners, two of whom had died. Page fed his guests well before driving them to a hotel where a military headquarters was being established to coordinate the evacuation of all the POW camps in the area.

The following day, Lush headed back to the camp at Ikuno to collect gear they had left behind and pick up Ken Trumble, who had remained behind. In Osaka, their transformation from prisoners of war to masters of a newly conquered nation would be complete.

Built in the 1930s, the New Osaka Hotel was one of the most luxurious hotels in Japan. Prewar brochures described it as "the centre of Japan, the centre of convenience". The Australians and the Americans soon turned it into their liberation palace. Lush took up residence in a suite where Japanese beer was soon being delivered by the crate: "Suddenly, here we were holding court in a beautiful suite with baths and hot water. It was like we had arrived in heaven."[4]

Lush soon got to work managing the hotel kitchen which fed the large numbers of men arriving at the centre each day and prepared food drops for those billeted at other places in the area. He put guards on the kitchen, creating a guard group "from amongst the fittest of the blokes". Ken Trumble worked with an American officer establishing a switchboard to connect phone lines to all of the outlying camps.

Soon after the Australians had joined in the takeover of the Osaka Hotel, a US Army 'recovery squad' arrived from Yokohama to co-ordinate the evacuation of all POWs in the area. The Australians were astonished at the sight of six female war correspondents who accompanied the team. "Dressed in slacks, shirts and standard army boots," John Paterson wrote in his diary. "Very efficient people they seemed to be."

Lush was interviewed by John Loughlin, a special correspondent of the Melbourne *Argus* who had landed in Japan with the British forces: "That night Loughlin sat down at the piano and played 'Roll Out the Barrel' and all these songs which had been popular during the war years but which we had never heard before. He also told us what had gone on whilst we were POWs. That was the first time we heard for certain that women were in the services and that there was rationing in Australia. He brought us up to date on so many of the things that happened since we had become prisoners back at the start of 1942."

In his dispatch to *The Argus*, Loughlin would marvel at the spectacle of the POW-led takeover of Osaka and at the leading role played by the 8th Division Signals officers including John Paterson, Doug Lush and Ken Trumble:

> From their stinking prison camps and detention barracks, where they had suffered months of misery, starvation and humiliations, US, Australian and British prisoners moved into the fashionable 800-room Osaka Hotel which became HQ of the prisoners' own evacuation scheme. Ex-prisoners lounged luxuriously in modern furnished suites with private bathrooms, and staffed the hotel themselves with rosters of cooks, waiters, reception desk attendants, clerks for handling new POW arrivals. They even had a spanking guard of Royal Marines armed with rifles seized from Japanese guards. While Japanese police and guards looked on helpless and bewildered, high-spirited POWs roamed the streets carrying long Japanese police swords, raided warehouses and carried away provisions to supplement food dropped by US planes. They completely took over the Japanese brewery to provide a constant supply of beer while awaiting their departure from Yokohama.[5]

While the Australian officers were finding their bearings in Osaka, many of their fellow former prisoners from Kobe were making their way from the Yoshikuma camp to Nagasaki in preparation for repatriation. Some of the newly freed coalminers would shock the Americans waiting to receive them, as Des Mulcahy recounted:

> We got word to catch this train and move down to the Nagasaki wharf. We loaded up and got on the train and down we went. I got out of the train and walked over and saluted the senior Yank I could see there and he looked a big perplexed. I said, 'What's the trouble sir?' He said, 'You gave me a fright … I was sent down here to meet a trainload of Aussies and when you got off

the train I thought it was black Americans.' I said, 'We've had 82 days on the coalmines, sir, without a break and no soap and no hot water' ... We went into the next hut and there were all hot showers, about 30 or 40 hot showers around the wall, and we had lashings of soap and hot water and we had a fantastic time with this. It was the best bath that I had ever had.[6]

After a week in Osaka, Doug Lush and Ken Trumble tired of the wait for repatriation and headed off to Yokohama to take their chances for a fast-tracked departure. Their luck was in, as Lush recounted: "When we arrived at Yokohama, the band was playing and there was just the two of us. There were a few Red Cross girls there as well. Here we were re-kitted out with American uniforms and they fed us up. Then we worked our way over to the airfield and got onto an American transport plane and went down to Okinawa."

At Okinawa, the main staging point beyond the Japanese mainland for prisoner repatriations, the men spent a couple days waiting before they were allocated seats aboard a convoy of Liberator transport planes ferrying former POWs to Manila. Their joy at finally departing Japan after almost three years in captivity was soon tempered by fresh tragedy, as Lush recounted: "From Okinawa we left in ten Liberators for Manila. It was the cyclone season and two of the Liberators were lost. One of the Liberators was transporting Major Houghton, who was the English officer in charge at the Ikuno camp, which was very unfortunate. Trumble and I had been separated and were aboard different aircraft. When we got to Manila we both thought the other hadn't arrived when they should have. We were pleased to catch up when we eventually found each other."

Twelve Australians had perished when their Liberator plunged into the sea off Formosa. Another five Australians died when the second aircraft crashed into the central mountains of the island. Among those killed was Sergeant Albert Arthur James, whose son Clive would become a celebrated writer and television presenter. The death of Major Alfred Houghton would be a second cruel blow for his widow Gladys, desperately awaiting his return to their home in Hornchurch, Essex. Their son George, a sub lieutenant with the Royal Naval Volunteer Reserve, had been killed on 10 June 1944 when the escort carrier HMS *Tracker* collided with a Canadian ship during D-day operations off the Irish coast.

In Manila, Lush and Trumble attended debriefing sessions over several days – "reporting our experiences and naming certain Japanese" – as the Americans began gathering information that would later underpin their war crimes trials. Lush then "very impulsively got an aircraft from there to Darwin". Trumble waited behind in Manila where he was soon reunited with John Paterson. Eventually, the pair made their way back to Australia together aboard the British aircraft carrier HMS *Formidable*.

Doug Lush would be one of the first Australian POWs from Japan to make it home. On his arrival in Darwin he was welcomed by the Chief Signals Officer. "He came out to meet me and said, 'Hello Lush' and then said, 'I will introduce you to my Staff Captain and she will look after you.' I said, 'Beg your pardon, Sir?' We didn't have women in uniform like that when I left Australia in 1941. I didn't know whether to salute her or kiss her. After I had washed up, she took me around to the Mess and I was the only male there. I was quite impressed but I was also a bit shy."

Lush spent a couple of days in Darwin, during which he was at last fitted out with a new Australian army uniform. He then boarded another Liberator for the final leg of his journey to home and freedom

– sleeping all the way to Sydney on a mattress in the bomb bay. For others who had shared the final months of captivity at Ikuno, the journey home would take a little longer.

Chapter 20

JUSTICE

It is a day which we Americans shall remember as a day
of retribution as we remember that other day,
the day of infamy.

President Harry Truman in a national broadcast on 'VJ Day',
1 September 1945

A week after the Japanese surrender, General Douglas MacArthur, Supreme Commander of the Allied Powers and the new de facto ruler of Japan, took the first step towards bringing justice – or retribution – for all the victims of Japanese war crimes across Asia and the Pacific since Pearl Harbor. He ordered the arrest of 39 of the most obvious suspects – predominantly members of General Hideki Tojo's war cabinet. On 19 January 1946 the International Military Tribunal for the Far East was established in Tokyo.

Eventually about 5600 Japanese would be prosecuted. Their cases were summarised as 'Class A' crimes (leaders who conspired to start and wage war), 'Class B' (conventional war crimes) and 'Class C' (crimes against humanity). More than 4400 would be convicted and 1000 of those hanged. Most of the Class B and C cases would be heard by a military commission of the US Eighth Army sitting in Yokohama. The long arrest lists for those accused of 'Class C' crimes of the abuse of prisoners of war would include Sergeant Yoshinari Minemoto and

Civilian Interpreter Kazuo Kobayashi. A chance meeting in Tokyo would save one of the two men who had shown kindness and humanity towards the prisoners at Tanagawa and Ikuno camps, but not the other.

As the most senior officer at Ikuno, and a survivor of the atrocities committed in the wake of the Japanese victory in the Philippines, Lieutenant Colonel Frank Fliniau was called to Tokyo after liberation to help prepare for the war crimes trials. In early December he appeared before the International Military Tribunal to give evidence about the bashing of American and Filipino POWs in Iloilo City.

One day while walking down a corridor in the Judge Advocate's offices at MacArthur's General Headquarters, Fliniau was stunned to encounter Kazuo Kobayashi, who had been brought in for questioning. "Fireball!" he exclaimed, "What are you doing here?" His astonishment was compounded by the fact that, before farewelling the interpreter at Ikuno, Fliniau had given Kobayashi a letter of commendation that he hoped would serve as a *laissez-passer* in the event that he was challenged by military police about his role at the camp:

> This is to introduce Mr Kobayashi, our interpreter at the Ikuno Prisoner of War Camp. Mr Kobayashi cooperated with all prisoners of war and it was through his cooperation that we were able to accomplish many things which would have been impossible without him. Mr Kobayashi purchased with his own money medicines in which we were in dire need of. He also kept us abreast of the news day by day thus keeping the morale of the men high. Mr Kobayashi's knowledge of English and the ways of the American people is a credit to him as an interpreter.[1]

Thirty minutes after their encounter, Fliniau emerged from a nearby office and told Kobayashi that he was to be released immediately. The next day, on the colonel's recommendation, he was given a job as an interpreter on the GHQ staff. Kobayashi could only marvel at his good fortune, as he later wrote:

> Though I have nothing at all to feel guilty about, I wonder what my fate would have been if I had not met Lieutenant Colonel Fliniau in that corridor at the Judge Advocate's Office. There might have been some who were put under suspicion and, unable to get any proper witnesses, were branded as convicts for charges of which they had not the faintest idea. Fortunately, I was set free right away because that good witness, Lieutenant Colonel Fliniau, just happened to be there. I savoured that paper-thin difference between heaven and hell.[2]

Kobayashi's luck would not be shared by his friend Sergeant Minemoto. Accused of being involved in the death of an American POW at the Tanagawa camp, Minemoto was convicted as a Class C war criminal and sentenced to 10 years' detention in the infamous Sugamo Jail in Tokyo where his fellow prisoners included Hideki Tojo, before the former prime minister was hanged in 1948. He would eventually be pardoned in 1951.

In April 1943 US Marines Private Everett Tyler had gone missing from the Tanagawa camp, as Colonel William Braly would recount in his war memoir *The Hard Way Home*. Tyler had become unbalanced as a result of severe mistreatment, prolonged starvation and exposure. Repeatedly he had been beaten for offences "no sane man would commit". The senior American officer at the camp had told the Japanese that Tyler was a hospital case and should not be sent out to work, but the appeal was ignored. Then one day Tyler disappeared from the camp. Being hungry, he stopped at the first house he came to and is believed to have asked for food. The astonished resident immediately raised the alarm. Guards soon arrived and took Tyler back to the camp where he was thrown into the guardhouse and beaten severely.

A couple of hours later, two men armed with long heavy sticks arrived at the guardhouse and proceeded to beat Tyler to death. His agonised screams could be plainly heard, but the camp commander ignored the pleas of the officer prisoners for him to be spared.[3]

As head of the camp administration, it had been Minemoto who, under orders from the commandant, had placed Tyler in the guard-house after his escape. According to Kobayashi, Minemoto had tried unsuccessfully to protect the prisoner: "The following day, Minemoto, in order to restrain the beatings the army sentries were giving the prisoner, walked into the struggling group of people and calmed the situation. After the war, however, a POW erroneously testified that Minemoto was there beating the prisoner and instructing others to do the same. Just on that single testimony, Minemoto was convicted of torturing a prisoner and sentenced to 10 years in prison."[4]

US Army Lieutenant Bob Broadwater was convinced of Minemoto's innocence. During a visit to Japan in 1984 he was shocked to learn of the conviction and later wrote to Kobayashi: "I heard after the war Mr Minemoto was sentenced as a war criminal and suffered a long time in Sugamo Prison. They say it was for torturing prisoners, but it's such a shame and I'm so sorry. I really think that judgement was in error. I can't remember him doing anything deserving of being tried like that."[5]

Broadwater also wrote a note to Minemoto expressing his regret that he unfairly had been "bearing the cross of a war criminal". As soon as he received it, Minemoto phoned Kobayashi "in a voice of elation": "I insisted on my innocence and tried to give my side of the story, but I couldn't get it across to them. All they did was push for a conviction, but I swore to God I was innocent. I'd like to express my gratitude to Mr Broadwater. What's past is past, but more than anything else it is so encouraging to know that there is an American still alive who can attest to my innocence. I feel as if I have met a saint."[6]

In the autumn of 1988, Kazuo Kobayashi would have a joyous reunion with his own patron saint. As he was ushered into the living room of a house in Nevada City, California, a tall, white-haired man – back in full military dress uniform for the occasion – stepped forward with a beaming smile. "Well, hello Fireball!" declared Frank Fliniau. "Thanks for coming." Kobayashi was overcome with emotion: "No words can express what happened next. We just stood there, hugging each other. We talked and talked while enjoying a home-cooked meal … and he told me, 'You and I owe each other our lives'."

Justice would not be delivered for the prisoners of the Kobe camp until almost three years after the war. On 28 June 1948, the Military Commission sitting in Yokohama sentenced Colonel Sotaro Murata – who had command of all POW camps in the Osaka region – to life imprisonment with hard labour. Captain Yasuji 'Bonnie Leslie' Morimoto – who controlled the Kobe camp – got 40 years with hard labour.

Murata was found not guilty of complicity in the death of Private Everett Tyler at Tanagawa camp – another of the camps under his control – but guilty of ordering the execution by lethal injection in July 1944 of US Marine Corporal Herbert Wharton and Marine Private Thomas McGee who had escaped briefly from the Sakuarajima camp in Osaka. He was also convicted of contributing to the death of Dutch prisoner Willem Wilsterman in the Kobe camp in December 1943.

Army Judge Advocate Lieutenant Colonel Allan Browne ruled that Murata had personally participated in the murder of the two American escapers and had "direct responsibility for two other deaths and for many beatings and killings plus instances of refusing available medical aid and forcing sick prisoners to work".[7] Browne found that Morimoto "was directly responsible for the permitting of the deaths of two POWs who were ostensibly under his protective mantle" and many other abuses. He too had contributed to the death of Wilsterman by ordering his "solitary confinement with insufficient food and without adequate heat or clothing for approximately 16 days".

The Australians named in the course of the trial whose abuse at the hands of Murata and Morimoto had contributed to their deaths included Robert Flanagan, Jack Russell, George Powell and Mervin Justice. In all, 18 Australians died at the Kobe camp, as well as 14 British and 19 Dutch prisoners.

In November 1948, the Yokohama military commission convicted the last and most egregious of the Japanese guards involved in the murder of Willem Wilsterman. Ko Nishikawa was found guilty of severely beating and mistreating more than 13 prisoners of war at Kobe camp, including Wilsterman and Doug Lush, and sentenced to eight years' hard labour. "The sentence of eight years is not considered excessive for this accused's brutal conduct. It is recommended that clemency be denied," Judge Advocate Browne ruled.[8]

The conviction and punishment of Nishikawa, Murata and Morimoto would be little comfort for the family of Willem Wilsterman, whose problems would be compounded by the collapse of Dutch control of the East Indies after the war and the upheaval that created the new nation of Indonesia. Margarethe Wilsterman-Herbig, now a widow with five children – son Henry and daughters Stenny, Mary, Orla and Ilka – decided to return to Surinam to settle. But they got little help from a Dutch bureaucracy overwhelmed by the war and its chaotic aftermath – despite Willem's supreme sacrifice in the service of the Dutch army.

The Dutch consulate in Surabaya refused to issue the family with exit visas to travel to the Netherlands, from where they hoped to journey on to Surinam. The family despaired before Mary, a plucky 16-year-old, decided to write a pleading letter to Queen Juliana. After the palace was spurred to respond, embarrassed consulate staff promptly issued the visas. But the family's arrival in the Netherlands would not be the end of their struggle. With little money, they ended up stranded in a small apartment in the northern Dutch city of Leeuwarden – an unheated room with not enough coal to fuel the stove and poor food. This time daughter Orla wrote to the queen. Soon the family had a house of their own in the neighbouring city of Groningen, where they decided to stay and where the children would complete their schooling.

It was not until early 2017 that Willem Wilsterman's sacrifice was finally, formally recognised by the Netherlands authorities. He was posthumously awarded the Dutch Mobilization War Cross.

Chapter 21

HOME

Only those who have been prisoners have any
conception of the horrors of being a prisoner
or of the insufferable joy of release.

P.C. Wren, Beggars' Horses

Homecoming would be bittersweet. When his flight touched down
at Sydney's Mascot airport on 25 September 1945, it had been more
than four and a half years since Doug Lush embarked for Malaya. He
had been changed by the traumas of war and captivity. Those at home
had changed too during the long and anxious separation.

Among those at the airport looking to meet returning loved ones
was Florence Johnson, the wife of Lieutenant Ralph Johnson. Johnson
had served on the 22 Brigade headquarters staff in Malaya with Lush
and had been with him on the journey from Singapore to Japan. Soon
after their arrival in Kobe, the two young officers had parted company.
When the Japanese decided to send some of the Australian officers to
another camp at Zentsuji on the island of Shikoku, among those chosen
were Ken Trumble and Bill Bathgate. But Johnson and Bathgate had
been good mates since they served as liaison officers with the brigade
back in Malaya, and were determined stay together, as Lush explained:
"Trumble wrote to the Japanese and said he was my cousin and he
would like to take Johnson's place. So they let Trumble remain. The

irony of it all was that Johnson and Bathgate went on to Zentsuji and Johnson died there soon after the war ended. He had just gone inside his hut to make a cup of tea when the Americans dropped 44-gallon drums of relief supplies and one came through the roof and killed him. When I flew into Sydney, Johnson's wife was there waiting to meet him. It was too soon to tell her that he had died as she had not yet been informed officially. It was a tragedy. He was a nice bloke."

From the airport, Lush was sent directly to Concord Military Hospital for a check-up. He was suffering stomach pains and the doctors soon confirmed that he had appendicitis. But, determined to get home as soon as possible, he decided to postpone the operation and headed straight to Sydney Central station where he boarded a train for Melbourne with "half a dozen other blokes". On their arrival at Spencer Street station there was no great fanfare for the returning officers, but a picture of Lush and his mates appeared in *The Age* newspaper the next day.

Ominously, Lush's wife Dorothy was not at the station to welcome him home. He was met instead by his aunt, who soon gave him the bad news. During their long separation, Dorothy had fallen in love with another man, no less than one of the most famous figures in Australian radio broadcasting.

Born in New Zealand, Jack Davey had by the early 1940s become Australia's highest paid and most popular radio personality. With his trademark greeting of "Hi ho, everybody", he hosted a nationally syndicated breakfast show, a daytime quiz and an evening variety program while also doing voiceover work for Fox Movietone newsreels. He was also a notorious gambler, wildly extravagant motor-racing enthusiast and voracious womaniser. According to his biographer and long-time producer Lew Wright, "He loved fast cars and glamorous women. Both had to have lines and looks. There was never any shortage of either."[1]

As the war unfolded, Davey had joined the American Red Cross as a field entertainer with the honorary rank of captain, taking shows to troops across Australia and the islands of the Pacific. During his travels, Davey met the glamorous Dorothy Lush who was soon being described in the newspapers as a former model and radio actress who now called herself Diana Chase.

Davey's first marriage had collapsed very publicly in 1941 when he walked out on his wife Dulcie and then sent her a note saying "Let's call it a day". He then moved into an apartment in the Sydney suburb of Vaucluse that he shared with the actor Errol Flynn. "It wasn't the only thing they shared," Lew Wright would later observe. "Both of them possessed an intense desire to wring all they could from life. They both loved the company of beautiful women."[2]

Doug Lush may have anticipated that his marriage was in trouble before his homecoming, if not the public magnitude of his repudiation. In late 1943, John Paterson, who constantly felt the separation from his wife and daughter, would write in his secret prison diary: "Lush says some funny things at times. He doesn't appear at all anxious to return to his wife but wants to continue his 'world tour'."[3]

But when confronted with Dorothy's infidelity, Doug Lush's response was forceful. The couple was divorced five months after Lush's return to Australia. In an undefended suit in the Melbourne courts, co-respondent Jack Davey was required to pay £550 in costs and damages to Doug Lush – the equivalent of a $40,000 settlement today. In the end, Lush received none of it. The funds mysteriously vanished in the hands of the lawyers.

Davey and his new partner wed in May 1947, but the relationship was soon heading in the same direction as Davey's first marriage. Within a few years, after the birth of a daughter, it too was over with "dramatic suddenness", according to Lew Wright: "The breakdown of his marriage ... resulted in a succession of badly chosen female alliances."[4] As the *Australian Dictionary of Biography* would note after Davey's death from lung cancer at the age of 52, in 1959: "Marriage had little effect on his way of life."

The stress of his divorce would not have helped Lush's efforts, along with his friends and fellow POWs, to readjust after the long years of deprivation, hardship and ill health. During his time as a POW, as well as the starvation and the frequent bashings, he had suffered from beri-beri, dengue fever, jaundice and sinusitis. Back home, he suffered blackouts, regular stomach upsets and chronic back pain. He would also display many symptoms of nervous disorder that would, a generation later, be recognised as post-traumatic stress. Readjusting to civilian life took a long time:

> Having three and a half years of what we were subjected to was like spending 20 years in Pentridge prison. We were deprived of everything. I guarantee half the blokes couldn't read and write for a while after liberation. When Ken Trumble and I were being evacuated from Japan we met these two American Red Cross workers, quite attractive women. I've never had trouble talking to women but I was so tongue tied I wasn't game to speak to them. It was shyness. We had been deprived of all these things for so long. I don't think anyone in Australia realised the depravity of the situation we had been through. It took us a while to get our lives back to normal.

John Paterson, who had stayed on in Osaka to assist the Americans coordinating the repatriation of Allied POWs, did not get home to

Australia until about a month after Doug Lush. He had flown from Yokohama to Okinawa aboard an American C47 Dakota whose pilot gave his passengers a scenic view of Tokyo and Mount Fuji. Bad weather forced them to land at Kanoya, near the southern tip of Kyushu island, and wait overnight. On reaching Okinawa the next day, he was reunited with many of the men he had been with at the Kobe camp who were among more than 4000 former POWs awaiting transport to Manila and home. The first person to greet him on arrival in Manila the following day was Trumble, who had arrived 13 days earlier. Soon after, Paterson was told that the next plane after his out of Okinawa had crashed. Among those killed were several men who had shared his tent the night before. While noting ruefully in his diary that this was the "luck of the draw", he immediately requested that the last leg of his journey home be made by sea. His wish was granted seven days later when the aircraft carrier HMS *Formidable* departed Manila, bound for Sydney with 1300 former POWs and internees aboard. Once they had embarked, the diary in which Paterson had painstakingly chronicled the travails of the previous four years, in more than 100,000 words, was ended.

There would be a special surprise in store for Ken Trumble when HMS *Formidable* arrived back in Australia on 6 December 1945 and he took one of the special trains ferrying the Victorian troops back to Melbourne. His twin brother Robert, recently promoted to captain after serving with the army in the Pacific, had been given a mysterious order to present himself at Melbourne's Spencer Street railway station. When the train pulled in, the brothers were joyously reunited after nearly five years apart, neither having expected to see the other.

Des Mulcahy, who had made his way from Nagasaki to Manila, was still enjoying the American hospitality – unlimited food, comfortable beds and free cigars – when his passage home was abruptly fast-tracked:

"I was there this morning and a bloke poked his head in the door and said, 'Is there a bloke by the name of Mulcahy here?' I said, 'Yes, who are you?' He said, 'My name is Lieutenant so and so and I am flying out of Tocumwal. Your old girlfriend is in charge of the WAAAF [Women's Auxiliary Australian Air Force] down there and she has had us looking for you for a fortnight. We are taking you home to get her off our back.' So next morning I had to go to headquarters and they flew me right home."[5]

The former girlfriend's kindness was not repaid. Soon after his return, Mulcahy visited a cousin in West Wyalong who had married a dentist. During his time as a POW, his jaw had been broken eight times from bashings by Japanese guards and many of his teeth were broken and crooked. His week in the dentist's chair would deliver much more than a new smile: "I went down this morning and got in the chair and looked up and this little vision sort of poked its head around and I said, 'Where did you come from?' She said, 'I am the assistant.' The next morning she was there again and I said, 'Where do you live?' I switched horses and became engaged to her, cancelled the other one, became engaged and married this one." It would be a very happy marriage that lasted for 50 years and produced eight children, four boys and four girls.

Paterson's homecoming was particularly memorable as his daughter Janet had grown from a child to a young woman in the five years he had been away, as she recalled: "It was such a big event for the family as we had not expected him to come back. During all the time he was away, my mother never talked to me about him. Every Sunday we went to lunch at my aunt's house and the wishbones from the chicken were kept in hope, but we didn't dare talk about the future. I was so excited when I went with Mum to the big army base to meet him. He

190

couldn't get over how tall I had grown. I remember we then took a house at the beach and Mum and Dad slept together in a single bed. I thought that was lovely."[6]

Ethel Paterson's sister Bessie had married into the Ballantyne family. Established in 1929, K.L. Ballantyne Pty Ltd – 'Produce Merchants, Food Canners and Exporters' – was and remains one of Melbourne's most successful privately owned companies, specialising in dairy products. Soon after his return from Japan, John Paterson joined the family firm and later became the company's overseas director, often travelling to Asia and the Middle East on business.

Soon after his return from Japan, Ken Trumble met and married Helen, with whom he would have three children – Michael, Hugh and Elizabeth. He returned to his job at ICI and quickly rose through the management ranks. In 1962 the family moved to Adelaide where Trumble was appointed ICI's state manager. They returned to Melbourne several years later when he took over the firm's alkali division. What many regarded as a career path destined for the top of the chemical company ended abruptly in 1966 when Ken Trumble suffered a severe heart attack and died. He was 47.

According to sons Michael and Hugh, Trumble bore no lasting enmity towards the Japanese and empathised with the suffering of ordinary Japanese people through the war that was not their making. His own suffering in captivity would have a lasting impact on his health. Before the war he had weighed 11 stone. When it ended he was just 6 stone. While the weight returned, his health remained fragile for the rest of his short life.

Doug Lush was formally discharged from the army on 14 March 1946. He returned to his job with Guardian Assurance, accepting an assignment as a country inspector, but he found it hard to settle:

I used to pass out when I was speaking to people; all of a sudden I would flop, just black out. I never told the office about it. I don't know what was the cause. A nervous condition, maybe, or something, but these sorts of things did happen to POWs and I think it took a while before the doctors could understand. In the end they said it would take you about three years to get over what had you had been through so don't expect to get back to normal before that. A lot of blokes just couldn't settle down.

The war had robbed Doug Lush of what might have been some of his best sporting years, but he soon returned to his beloved athletics and hockey. His athletics team, the Melbourne Harriers, had been 'A' Grade Premiers in 1939 and runners up in 1940. By 1946, the team had been relegated to 'C' grade and a number of members had been lost in the war. Lush resumed his training with enthusiasm. While travelling with work to different parts of Victoria every week, often to remote country areas, he was unable to train regularly with the squad but would make time to train on his own. In the 1948 Victorian championships he ran second to Ray Weinberg, of rival club St Stephen's Harriers. Weinberg would go on to compete at the London and Helsinki Olympic Games and, in 1952, recorded the world's fastest time for the 220-yard hurdles.

Shortly before the fall of Singapore, Lush had been told by his superiors that he had been promoted to the rank of captain. But, amid the chaos of the final days before the surrender, the paperwork was never completed. The loss of seniority, and pay, was a gnawing irritation throughout his time as a POW. It became a major resentment when, after his return to Australia, his efforts to have the promotion confirmed were brusquely dismissed by military bureaucrats who could find no formal records about the appointment.

Lush had also been recommended for a military decoration for his "courage and devotion to duty" by Brigadier Charles Kappe, who had written: "He commanded an Infantry Brigade, Signal Section, with efficiency, courage and great cheerfulness. During the Battle of Singapore, the Brigade to which he was attached received the first Japanese onslaught and remained in contact, fighting desperately day and night for a week. During this period, Mr Lush remained on duty to the point of exhaustion, setting a great example to his men and those associated with him."[7]

To Kappe's "great disappointment", no award was made. For Lush, these rebuffs became emblematic of the authorities' reluctance to properly acknowledge the sacrifice of the men – and the lasting wounds, physical and emotional, that they came home with: "John Paterson never really got the accolades he deserved. Running a camp of six hundred men for two and a half years at Kobe, with all the problems we had, he did a marvellous job and there was no recognition at all. I recommended him for an OBE and they wiped that off and I know he recommended me for a Mention in Despatches or whatever and nothing ever came of it."

John Paterson also resented the fact that the years of imprisonment had denied him the natural progression to his 'majority' – the rank of major. By the end of the war he had held the rank of captain – in the militia and the regular army – for an extraordinary 19 years. But while an imperial honour eluded him, he was awarded the army's Efficiency Decoration in October 1946 in recognition of his wartime leadership. Ken Trumble was awarded the lesser army Efficiency Medal in 1952.

Soon after returning home, Lush would begin what became a lifetime commitment to supporting the widows and families of those men who had not made it back. He became president and later patron of the 8th Division Signals Association and devoted considerable time to the association's welfare work supporting families in need. At the outset, he wrote many letters to widows recounting details of their husbands' and sons' war service and time in captivity. One of those he supported was the widow of Signalman William Constable who died in May 1945. Martha Constable lived in Castlemaine and every year for the rest of Doug Lush's life she would send him a card at Christmas and a tin of the famous Castlemaine Rock toffee.

In their work with the families, Lush and the other surviving POWs would always be circumspect about describing the final days of those who perished:

> We learned to keep the details about how some of our men had died whilst in captivity to ourselves. By the time we got back, these families already knew that their sons and husbands were lost and it felt like it was opening up old wounds for these relatives if we spoke too much to them about what had happened. We felt it should be left that their loved ones had died as a prisoner of war. If we had gone into the actual details of these deaths, nothing good could come out of it. Some of the families of those who died with us at Kawasaki had themselves already passed away whilst we had been away, so there was no-one left to mourn for some of our fellows.

Doug Lush and John Paterson would remain firm friends for the rest of their lives. They would attend together every home game of their beloved Essendon Football Club, striding in step to seats A1 and A2, held permanently in reserve for them in the grandstand at Windy Hill. When John's daughter Janet married, Lush spoke at the wedding. And Lush would be present, years later, at the Heidelberg Repatriation Hospital when, a week after suffering a major heart attack, Paterson passed away.

Several years after his return from Japan, Lush met Elsa May Clarke, a senior buyer at the Myer department store, while holidaying at Lorne. They married in May 1952 and their only son, Stewart, was born the following year. Unlike Lush's first marriage, it would be a happy union that endured for 59 years until Elsa's death in 2011. Doug died, at the age of 97, in September 2015.

The experience of war would remain a powerful undercurrent throughout Doug Lush's long and prosperous life, during which he would build a very successful insurance company of his own. And while time healed many wounds, he could never forget the many atrocities committed by the Japanese. Like many of his army mates, he had little time for arguments that the nuclear attacks on Hiroshima and Nagasaki – and the earlier and much more deadly firebombing of other Japanese cities – was a disproportionate response by the Americans: "I know if it had happened in Australia we would be up in arms over the whole thing, but it brought the war to an end and it brought an end to all the terrible things the Japanese military had done. How could they have done what they did? Remember, for example, poor old Captain John Park and the three others from the 2/9th Field Ambulance. It belies all belief as to what makes these fellows tick."

John Park had been a close friend of Lush from their Melbourne athletics days in the late 1930s. Park was on the Australian team at the 1938 Empire Games in Sydney, where he won a silver medal. On 9 February 1942, shortly before the fall of Singapore, Park had led a small field ambulance team towards Kranji, on the north of the island, where they planned to set up a forward dressing station. They were not heard from again. Retreating Australian troops later reported seeing an ambulance overturned beside the main road into the area. Four months later, a working party of Australian POWs found a shallow grave and Park's identity discs. The grave contained four bodies – all with their hands tied behind their backs and all decapitated.[8]

Lush was equally and abidingly outraged by the massacre of many of his friends from the Australian Army Nursing Service on Banka Island in 1942: "I resent very much the attitude of the Japanese to our women and what they did to our nurses. I can't forgive them for that and I never will forgive them for that. It is on my mind all the time. To think that these barbarians would go and do what they did. I despise them. I really do."[9]

Despite his abiding contempt for what the Japanese had done during the war, Lush had wanted to return in peacetime to the country of his captivity, but never did. The war had given him a taste for rice and Japanese food. Once, while a patient at Melbourne's Cabrini Hospital, a Japanese nurse asked whether he knew much about her country. "When I was younger, I spent a bit of time there," he replied, without elaborating.

Many of the ex-POWs would make return visits to Japan in the years after the war. For some it helped lay the demons to rest, and soften the bitterness towards the nation that had stolen so much of their youth. Jack Chapman took his brother Bob on a holiday to Japan after he retired. It transformed Bob's lingering hatred: "We went to Tokyo and took the bullet train and never mentioned the war. It was wonderful, a great experience, and it changed my mind. We could do what we liked. The Japanese took us everywhere. We were drinking with them and I got pretty full. One of them took me back to the hotel and put me to bed."[10]

Tomas Francis Murphy was just 15 years old when he lied about his age and stole his brother's name to enlist with the 8th Division Signals in 1941. 'Spud' Murphy, as he was known to all, would survive war, capture and the long years working in the Kawasaki shipyard and the Yoshikuma coal mine to return home a year before his 21st birthday. For years he was haunted by his wartime experiences and kept a Japanese sword under his bed, fearing a danger to his wife and family that he could never define.

In the late 1960s, Spud took three months off work to revisit all the places he had been during the war, including retracing the long march into captivity at Changi, this time wearing a suit. It was an emotional but cathartic experience. At Takatori Michi, site of the Kobe camp, he was sitting on a bench meditating on the past when he was approached by an elderly Japanese woman. On discovering that he had been a POW, she thanked him for saving her house on the night of 16 March 1945 when the city was razed by the US firebombing and the prisoners fought alongside their jailers to defend the neighbourhood. The woman then gave him some daphne cuttings and said, "You take them home to Australia and plant them and think of a grateful lady."[11]

On November 2005, the Murphy family hosted a cocktail reception in the West Tower Suite on the 35th floor of Melbourne's Sofitel Hotel to celebrate the life and 80th birthday of Spud. The room was filled with former POWs and their wives and partners, including Doug and Elsa Lush. There were speeches and a video but the guest of honour was not present, although perhaps he was in spirit. Murphy had died in 1998 at the age of 72.

In response to an article about Murphy's life published in *The Age* shortly before the reception, Keith Ross of Ripponlea wrote a letter to the editor recalling how he and his friend Jack Fitzgerald had also lied about their ages to enlist in the Second AIF, Ross being just 14 years and 11 months old and Fitzgerald 15 years and three months: "Jack served in the Middle East, I served in the Middle East and New

Guinea, and Tommy went to Singapore where he was surrendered to
the Japanese ... None of us had an easy time, but we did not suffer
the dreadful brutalities that decent, honourable men endured for three
years without relief. They were a special breed."[12]

They were indeed.

ROLL OF HONOUR

Osaka Number 5-D Camp (Kawasaki-Juko, Kobe)

Established as the Kobe Kawasaki Branch Camp of the Osaka Prisoner of War Camp on 8 December 1942 at 2-chime, Mariana-cho, Niagara-ku, Kobe city.

Renamed the Osaka Number 5 Branch Camp on 18 February 1943.

Renamed the Osaka Number 5 Dispatched Camp on 25 October 1943.

Closed on 21 May 1954.

A total of 51 Australian, British and Dutch POWs died at the camp or while working at the nearby shipyard of the Kawasaki Heavy Industry Company.

AUSTRALIAN

BEAVIS, George Alexander Walter VX57790 (Signalman, 8th Division Signals) 24 March 1945

CRITTENDEN, Henry Ernest NX33947 (Lance Corporal, 2/19th Battalion AIF) 1 November 1943

DAVIS, Eric Ronald NX60438 (Private, 2/19th Battalion AIF) 28 March 1943

DODDS, George NX73684 (Private, 2/19th Battalion AIF) 20 May 1943

DUNNE, George NX66214 (Private, 2/10 Field Ambulance AIF) 15 March 1943

FLANAGAN, Robert QX16297 (Lance Corporal, 8th Division
Signals) 21 May 1943

HALLAWAYS, Dennis NX73492 (Private, 2/19th Battalion AIF)
1 May 1943

HEYWOOD, James Alexander NX20271 (Private, 2/19th
Battalion AIF) 19 April 1943

INGRAM, Robert Cuthbert NX29000 (Signalman, 8th Division
Signals) 24 April 1944

JUSTICE, Mervin Charles NX58986 (Private, 2/19th Battalion
AIF) 18 April 1943

LYNCH, William Francis NX71578 (Signalman, 8th Division
Signals) 13 October 1944

McQUEEN, John Alan VX26878 (Signalman, 8th Division
Signals) 24 April 1943

MOESSINGER, Leslie James QX23316 (Private, 2/19th Battalion
AIF) 26 April 1943

MUSSETT, Harold Vivian NX35279 (Private, 2/19th Battalion
AIF) 24 October 1943

POWELL, George Ward NX20044 (Lance Sergeant, 8th Division
Signals) 2 March 1944

PRESS, Aubrey Daniel NX57672 (Private, 2/19th Battalion AIF)
1 May 1943

ROBINSON, William Robert NX60240 (Signalman, 8th Division
Signals) 22 November 1943

RUSSELL, Jack William NX69463 (Signalman, 8th Division
Signals) 24 February 1944

BRITISH

ANDREW, William Henry (Chief Petty Officer, Royal Navy)
22 March 1943

ANKERS, John Ashley (Lance Corporal, The Loyal Regiment –
North Lancashire) 28 April 1944

BRECK, Albert Henry (Private, Royal Army Medical Corps)
21 August 1943

DAUBNEY, Dennis (Sapper, Royal Engineers) 1 August 1945

FORD, William Benjamin (Warrant Officer Class 2, Royal
Engineers) 3 March 1945

GRAHAM, Eric Gordon Rishworth (Gunner, Royal Field
Artillery) 29 December 1943

HARNESS, Jack (Gunner, Royal Field Artillery) 22 June 1944

HOWARD, Frederick Joseph (Private, The Loyal Regiment –
North Lancashire) 3 January 1945

MILNE, Harry Russell (Gunner, Royal Field Artillery) 10 June 1944

OULTON, Frank (Private, The Loyal Regiment – North
Lancashire) 18 March 1944

SMITHIES, Archbell (Private, The Loyal Regiment – North
Lancashire) 13 January 1944

TAYLOR, Edward (Sergeant, The Loyal Regiment – North
Lancashire) 27 December 1943

WADE, Richard Woodcock (Gunner, Royal Field Artillery)
15 November 1944

WILSON, Raymond (Lance Bombardier, Royal Field Artillery)
29 January 1944

DUTCH

BEMMEL van, Marinus Joannes Petrus (Leading Seaman)
6 November 1943

BOTTGER, Alexander Hubert (Sergeant) 26 April 1943

DEUX, F.F. (Private First Class) 5 July 1943

EIJNWACHTER, Johan Cornelis (Quartermaster) 24 April 1943

GEELHOED, F.E. (Private First Class) 16 April 1943

KOK, Tonny (Private First Class) 4 January 1944

LEBERT, Johan Raymond Anyonie (Private First Class) 17 March
1943

MASSELINK, Johan (Sub Lieutenant) 27 April 1943

MEERCAMP van, Embden Johannes (Reserve Sub Lieutenant,
Special Services) 22 October 1944

MORBECK, Carlos (Seaman) 24 October 1944

NIJPJES, Teunis Marinus (Corporal) 18 January 1944

ORNEE, P.B. (Staff Sergeant) 22 March 1943

SACHS, Johannes (Staff Sergeant) 13 March 1943

SCHATTEVOET, Willem John (rank unknown) 2 April 1943

SCHEPENS, Jan Willem (Corporal) 3 April 1943

SCHREUDER, Fredrick Carel (Corporal) 16 April 1944

STREEFKERK, Johannes Jacobiu (Private First Class) 14 March
1943

WILLEMSEN, Dirk (Private First Class) 11 October 1944

WILSTERMAN, Willem Hendrik Louis (Private First Class)
15 December 1943

ACKNOWLEDGMENTS

This book would not have happened without the determination of Doug Lush to record the story of his wartime experiences and those of his comrades from the Signals Corps and the men of C Force. Over several years before his death in September 2015, Doug spent many hours setting down his thoughts and recollections in commissioned interviews with historian Carl Johnson. At the same time, he gathered copies of the unpublished diaries and memoirs of many of the men who had shared his experiences of war and captivity. That priceless archive of original, first-person accounts became the basis for this book. While sadly Doug would not live to see the fruit of his labours, his son Stewart was committed to seeing the project through to completion. I acknowledge his steadfast support and friendship over the past three years, and the assistance of his wife Jenny and son John.

Many other people supported my research and I am grateful particularly to the families of John Paterson, Ken Trumble, Lloyd Ellerman, Jack Chapman and Mick Kildey.

Captain John Paterson's secret diary – meticulously kept from the fall of Singapore until his journey home, at considerable personal risk – became an invaluable resource and roadmap for this narrative. The burden of leadership compounded the daily challenges of survival faced by every POW. John's courage and tenacity, and that of his fellow officers, in the face of relentless deprivation and abuse undoubtedly improved the miserable lot of his fellow Australian, British and Dutch prisoners. My thanks to Janet Paterson AM for sharing her memories of war and peace, and for permission to draw heavily on her father's diary and photographs.

Until the late stages of writing, my exhaustive efforts to make contact with the family of Lieutenant Ken Trumble had drawn a frustrating blank. In finally tracking down a possible phone number in the eastern suburbs of Melbourne, I was thrilled when the man who answered was Hugh Trumble, Ken's son and, of course, grandson of the cricketing legend. More exciting still was the news that the family had a copy of Ken's wartime diary. I am indebted to both Hugh and his brother Michael for sharing their family history and photos and for helping answer my many questions.

Peter Chapman and his sisters gave great assistance in tracking down wartime photographs of their father. Jack Chapman's memoirs, first assembled as a hand-bound typed manuscript in the 1990s, were lovingly transformed by his children into the glossy publication *The Life and Style of Jack Chapman*. It is a wonderful personal account of war and captivity told with spirit and humour. The book would carry the note: 'Jack Frederick Chapman 1922–2022 (?)'. Sadly, Jack wasn't able to deliver on this ambitious forecast, passing away in 2017 at the age of 94. In first making contact with the Chapman family, I was delightfully surprised to discover that Jack's elder brother and fellow POW, Bob, was alive and well and living nearby in suburban Melbourne. An afternoon chatting with Bob enriched my understanding of the POW experience in Japan – and how the bond between the two brothers helped them both to survive their ordeal.

My thanks to Lloyd Ellerman's son Peter, and Peter's wife Kathy, for their great help in sharing details of Lloyd's wartime memoir and family photos. Thanks also to Deborah Kelly for providing the portrait of her father, Mick Kildey – one of the great characters of C Force – and permission to draw from his account of life as a prisoner in Japan.

ACKNOWLEDGMENTS

From South Carolina, First Lieutenant Oel Johnson's daughter Olinda Major shared photographs and family records of her father's remarkable wartime experiences in the Philippines and Japan, and those of Oel's great friend Bob Broadwater who had championed the innocence of Sergeant Minimoto after he was imprisoned for 10 years for alleged war crimes.

Early in my research, looking for details about the Adam Park camp, I found a website featuring drawings done by one of the POWs. I soon realised that Robert Boyed Mitchell – Private Bob Mitchell from Marrickville NSW – was not only one the Australian signallers captured after the fall of Singapore but also a member of C Force and part of the group under Captain Paterson that would be sent to Kobe and later Fukuoka. Mitchell had begun sketching at Adam Park and continued through the years in Japan. Despite the deprivations of captivity, he was fascinated by the Japanese landscape and empathised with the plight of many ordinary Japanese. He kept his drawings hidden under the cardboard base of his Army-issue pack. The discovery of the secret artwork would have led to a severe beating, or worse, but Mitchell had discovered a talent and a passion that would lead him to a career as a professional artist after the war. My early attempts to make contact with Bob's family were fruitless. While assembling the images for the book, I made one last attempt. An old press cutting about a posthumous exhibition of Bob's work at Sydney's Mossman Art Gallery led me to a contact for his niece and fellow artist, Suzanne Alexander. My great thanks to Suzanne and Gordon Alexander for permission to reproduce a number of Bob's drawings – which he coloured after the war – and the photograph of Bob and his sister Nell.

Thanks to Taeko Sasamoto and her colleagues at the POW Research Network Japan (www.powresearch.jp) for providing details of all of the prisoners who died at the Kobe camp. The Network, a private citizens group, has done outstanding work over the past 20 years compiling and preserving the records of Allied prisoners held during the war and assisting veterans and researchers. Thanks also to the Netherlands Embassy in Canberra and to Riccardo Sietsma at the Netherlands Institute of Military History for translating the ranks and titles of the Dutch prisoners who died at Kobe.

I would also like to acknowledge David Fisher, my friend and eternal help desk; Griselda Molemans, for guiding my research into the life of Willem Wilsterman; and David Poulton, who first connected me with Stewart Lush.

The staff at Monash University Publishing have been a wonderful support, particularly during the trying months of pandemic lockdown in Victoria. My thanks in particular to director Greg Bain, publishing coordinator Jo Mullins and senior marketing coordinator Sarah Cannon. Editor John Mahony did an impressive job finessing the manuscript. Any errors that remain are all mine.

And finally, thanks to my wife Asil, and our children Emre and Serin, who have yet again endured my solitary adventures down the winding path of authorship with love and forbearance.

Mark Baker
Melbourne
September 2020

NOTES

Prelude

1   Doug Lush, Oral history interview (Lush family papers).
2   US Eighth Army war crimes verdict, Case 316 (Ko Nishikawa), Yokohama, 22 November 1948.
3   Australians at War Film Archive, University of NSW, Desmond Mulcahy interview, 2 May 2003.
4   Australian War Memorial archive, 'General information about Australian prisoners of the Japanese'.

Chapter 1: Brothers in Arms

1   John Paterson family private papers.
2   Tom Uren, *A Tribute to Jim Cairns*, October 2003 (Evatt Foundation).
3   Interview with Doug Lush, *We Survived the Hell Ships* video.

Chapter 2: To War

1   J.W. Jacobs & R.J. Bridgland, *Through: The Story of Signals 8 Australian Division*, pp. 2–3.
2   Ibid., p. 5.
3   Ibid., p. 26.
4   Lionel Wigmore, *The Japanese Thrust*, p. 60.
5   Ian Shaw, *On Radji Beach*, p. 16.
6   Lloyd Ellerman, *Memoirs*, p. 5.
7   Jacobs & Bridgland, p. 35.
8   Roger Maynard, *Hell's Heroes*, p. 37.
9   Jacobs & Bridgland, p. 39.
10 Shaw, p. 216.
11 Jacobs & Bridgland, p. 73.
12 Maynard, p. 43.
13 Jacobs & Bridgland, p. 77.

Chapter 3: The Fall

1   Rohan Rivett, *Behind Bamboo*, p. vii.
2   Masanobu Tsuji, *Singapore: The Japanese Version*, p. 95.
3   Wigmore, p. 103.
4   Mark Clisby, *Guilty or Innocent: The Gordon Bennett Case*, p. 11.
5   VeteransSA website: 75th Anniversary of the Battle of Gemas.
6   Cliff Whitelocke, *Gunners in the Jungle*, p. 65.

7   Anderson to Wigmore, notes on draft official history. AWM67 3/9 part one.
8   Mulcahy, Film Archive interview.
9   Jacobs & Bridgland, pp. 97–8.
10 Gordon Bennett, *Why Singapore Fell*, p. 161.
11 Ian Stewart, *History of the 2nd Argylls*, p. 99.
12 Ellerman, p. 11.
13 Stewart Lush, Eulogy for Doug Lush, Lush family papers.

Chapter 4: Captured

1   Wigmore, p. 283.
2   Tsuji, pp. 213–14.
3   Mulcahy, Film Archive interview.
4   Wigmore, p. 302.
5   Peter Thompson, *The Battle for Singapore*, p. 271
6   Wigmore, p. 308.
7   Clisby, p. 19.

Chapter 5: Changi

1   Jim Jacobs, *The Burma Railway: One Man's Story*, p. 4.
2   Mulcahy, Film Archive interview.
3   Clifford Kinvig, *Scapegoat: General Percival of Singapore*, p. 221.
4   Jacobs, p. 10.

Chapter 6: Adam Park

1   Jon Cooper, *Tigers in the Park*, book cover notes.
2   Ellerman, p. 11.
3   Australian War Memorial collection.
4   Jack Chapman, *The Life and Style of Jack Chapman*, p. 30.
5   Jim Hardacre, *The Lionel Matthews Story*, p. 10.

Chapter 7: C Force

1   Chapman, p. 42.
2   Ellerman, p. 22.
3   John Paterson, war diary, 4 December 1942, Paterson family papers.
4   Ibid., 6 December 1942.
5   Ibid., 8 December 1942.

Chapter 8: Kobe

1   Ellerman, p. 22.
2   Wigmore, p. 620.
3   Jacobs & Bridgland, p. 256.
4   Mick Kildey memoirs, p. 1.
5   Ken Trumble, war diary 9/10 December 1942.

6   Ellerman, p. 24.
7   Mulcahy, Film Archive interview.

Chapter 9: Kawasaki

1   Chapman, p. 46.
2   Spang & Wippich, *Japanese–German Relations 1895–1945*, p. 162.
3   Ellerman, p. 55.
4   Mulcahy, Film Archive interview.
5   http://230battalion.org.au/.
6   Kildey, p. 2.
7   Ibid., p. 3.
8   Chapman, p. 51.
9   Ibid.
10   Ellerman, p. 26.
11   Bob Chapman, interview with author.
12   Ibid.
13   Ellerman, p. 55.
14   Paterson diary, 22 May 1943.

Chapter 10: Sickness

1   Chapman, p. 47.
2   Ellerman, p. 28.
3   Signalman J.T. Bromley account to Doug Lush, Lush family papers.
4   Ibid.
5   Ellerman, p. 22.
6   Corporal J.F. Nicholls account to Doug Lush, Lush family papers.
7   Ibid.
8   Paterson diary, 20 July 1943.
9   Ibid., 7 November 1943.

Chapter 11: Hunger

1   Paterson diary, 29 March 1944.
2   Chapman, p. 54
3   Ibid., p. 63.
4   Kildey, p. 6.

Chapter 12: Violence

1   Paterson diary, 30 August 1943.
2   Chapman, p. 36.
3   Paterson diary, 9 August 1943.
4   Ibid.
5   Chapman, p. 36.
6   Paterson diary, 12 June 1943.

7   Interview with Doug Lush, *We Survived the Hell Ships* video.
8   Chapman, p. 49.
9   Kildey, p. 19.
10 Chapman, p. 49.
11 Mulcahy, Film Archive interview.
12 Paterson diary, 22 March 1944.
13 Ellerman, p. 30.

Chapter 13: News

1   Chapman, p. 54.
2   Paterson diary, 17 April 1944.
3   Chapman, p. 35.
4   Paterson diary, 19 April 1944.
5   *The Blackpool Gazette*, 4 March 2016.
6   Mulcahy, Film Archive interview.
7   Kildey, p. 4.
8   Ellerman, p. 32.
9   Chapman, p. 37.
10 Ellerman, p. 17.
11 http://forces-war-records.co.uk/.
12 Ibid.
13 Chapman, p. 54.
14 Kildey, p. 23.
15 Ellerman, p. 34.

Chapter 14: Santa

1   Jacobs & Bridgland, p. 248.
2   Kildey, p. 6.

Chapter 15: Fire

1   Paul Ham, *Hiroshima and Nagasaki*, p. 482.
2   Ibid., p. 176.
3   Ibid., p. 60.
4   Paterson diary, 17 March 1945.
5   Ibid.
6   Chapman, p. 41.

Chapter 16: Ikuno

1   Kazuo Kobayashi, *The POW and the Interpreter* (1989), US–Japan Dialogue on POWs, p. 5.
2   Paterson diary, 30 March 1945.
3   Oel Johnson, *The Coca-Cola Bottler* magazine, March 1946.
4   Kobayashi, p. 1.

5   Ibid., p. 2.
6   Ibid., p. 6.

Chapter 17: Yoshi

1   Ellerman, p. 38.
2   Bob Chapman, interview with the author.
3   Paul Heinrichs, 'A Look that Spoke of Horror', *The Age*, 7 August 2005.
4   'Australian War Slaves', *New Matilda*, 31 May 2006.
5   Ibid.
6   Athol Hill, Affidavit Fukuoka Number 26, http://mansell.com/ (Centre for Research Allied POWs Under the Japanese).
7   Ellerman, p. 39.
8   Ibid.
9   Mulcahy, Film Archive interview.

Chapter 18: Liberation

1   Harry S. Truman Library & Museum.
2   Ham, p. 223.
3   Ibid., p. 291.
4   Stephen Walker, *Shockwave*, pp. 90–91.
5   Paterson diary, 6 August 1945.
6   Peter Winstanley, *Prisoners of War of the Japanese 1942–45*, http://pows-of-japan.net/.
7   Paterson diary, 16 August 1945.
8   Trumble war diary, 16 August 1945.
9   Kobayashi, p. 7.
10   Paterson diary, 23 August 1945.
11   Chapman, p. 48.
12   Kildey, p. 7.
13   Ellerman, p. 44.
14   Trumble war diary, 28 August 1945.
15   Mulcahy, Film Archive interview.
16   Ibid.
17   Paterson diary, 30 August 1945.
18   Ibid., 2 September 1945.

Chapter 19: Osaka

1   Paterson diary, 5 September 1945.
2   Ibid.
3   Melbourne *Herald Sun*, 8 August 2005.
4   Ibid.
5   John Loughlin, 'From Camp Misery to Luxury', *The Argus*, September 1945.
6   Mulcahy, Film Archive interview.

Chapter 20: Justice

1 Kobayashi, p. 8.
2 Ibid., p. 9.
3 William Braly, *The Hard Way Home*, p. 229.
4 Kobayashi, p. 10.
5 Ibid.
6 Ibid.
7 Murata Case Number 155, Yokohama War Crimes Tribunal, 16 February 1949.
8 Ibid.

Chapter 21: Home

1 Lew Wright, 'The Man Who Was Jack Davey', *Australian Women's Weekly*, 15 October 1969.
2 Lew Wright, *The Jack Davey Story*, p. 34.
3 Paterson diary, 27 September 1943.
4 Wright, pp. 243–44.
5 Mulchay, Film Archive interview.
6 Janet Paterson, interview with the author.
7 Charles Kappe, letter of reference, Lush family papers.
8 Ian Shaw, *On Radji Beach*, p. 118.
9 Doug Lush, *Some Came Home* video documentary interview, 2014.
10 Bob Chapman, interview with the author.
11 Paul Heinrichs, 'A Look that Spoke of Horror', *The Age*, 7 August 2005.
12 *The Sunday Age*, 14 August 2005.

BIBLIOGRAPHY

Armstrong, Ralph H.E. *Short Cruise on the Vyner Brooke*, George Mann of Maidstone (2003).

Bennett, H. Gordon. *Why Singapore Fell*, Angus & Robertson (1944).

Braddon, Russell. *The Naked Island*, Werner Laurie (1952).

Braly, William C. *The Hard Way Home*, Washington Infantry Journal Press (1947).

Caulfield, Michael (Ed.). *War behind the Wire: Australian Prisoners of War*, Hachette (2008).

Chapman, Jack. *The Life and Style of Jack Chapman*, Blurb (2011).

Clisby, Mark. *Guilty or Innocent? The Gordon Bennett Case*, Allen & Unwin (1992).

Cooper, Jon. *Tigers in the Park: The Wartime History of Adam Park*, The Literary Centre, Singapore (2016).

Dandie, Alexander. *The Story of J Force*, privately published (1994).

Daws, Gavan. *Prisoners of the Japanese*, Scribe (2004).

Grehan, John & Mace, Martin. *Disaster in the Far East 1940–1942*, Pen & Sword (2015).

Hardacre, Captain J.F. *The Lionel Matthews Story*, private publication (1994).

Ham, Paul. *Hiroshima and Nagasaki: The Real Story of the Atomic Bombings and their Aftermath*, St Martin's Press (2011).

Kent Hughes, W.S. *Slaves of the Samurai*, Oxford University Press (1946).

Kinvig, Clifford. *Scapegoat: General Percival of Singapore*, Brassey's Biographies (1996).

Jacobs, J.W. & Bridgland, R.J. *Through: The Story of Signals 8 Australian Division*, 8 Division Signals Association (1949).

Jeffrey, Betty. *White Coolies*, Angus & Robertson (1954).

Martin, David E. & Gynn, Roger W.H. *The Olympic Marathon*, Human Kinetics, Illinois (2000).

Matthews, David. *The Duke: A Hero's Hero at Sandakan*, Seaview Press (2008).

Maynard, Roger. *Hell's Heroes: The Forgotten Story of the Worst POW Camp in Japan*, Harper Collins (2009).

Moreman, John & Reid, Richard. *A Bitter Fate: Australians in Malaya and Singapore, December 1941 – February 1942*, Department of Veterans' Affairs (2017).

Nelson, Hank. *Prisoners of War: Australians under Nippon*, ABC Books (1985).

Rivett, Rohan. *Behind Bamboo*, Angus & Roberston (1946).

Shaw, Ian W. *On Radji Beach*, Macmillan (2010).

Silver, Lynette. *Angels of Mercy*, Sally Milner Publishing (2019).

Simon, Jessie Elizabeth. *While History Passed*, William Heinemann (1954).

Simson, Ivan. *Singapore: Too Little, Too Late*, Asia Pacific Press (1970).

Smith, Colin. *Singapore Burning: Heroism and Surrender in World War II*, Penguin (2006).

Spang, Christopher & Wippich, Rolf-Harald. *Japanese–German Relations 1895–1945*, Routledge (2006).

Stewart, Ian. *The History of the 2nd Argylls: The Malayan Campaign 1941–42*, Thomas Nelson & Son (1947).

Thompson, Peter. *The Battle for Singapore: The True Story of the Greatest Catastrophe of World War II*, Little, Brown (2006).

Tsuji, Masanobu. *Singapore, the Japanese Version: Japan's Greatest Victory – Britain's Worst Defeat* (Translator: Margaret E. Lake), Ure Smith, Sydney (1960).

Walker, Stephen. *Shockwave: Countdown to Hiroshima*, Harper Collins (2005).

Wall, Don. *Singapore and Beyond*, 2/20 Battalion Association (1985).

Warren, Alan. *Singapore: Britain's Greatest Defeat*, Talisman (2002).

Wigmore, Lionel. *The Japanese Thrust*, Australian War Memorial (1957).

Whitelocke, Cliff. *Gunners in the Jungle: A Story of the 2/15 Field Regiment*, 2/15 Field Regiment Association, Sydney (1983).

Wright, Lew. *The Jack Davey Story*, Ure Smith (1961).

Wright, Lew. 'The Man Who Was Jack Davey'. *Australian Women's Weekly* (15 October 1969).

Unpublished Private Memoirs, Manuscripts and Diaries

Ellerman, Lloyd. *Memoirs of Lloyd Ellerman* (1986). Private collection of Ellerman family.

Gigger, Arthur. Interview with Lieutenant Colonel Peter Winstanley (2007), http://pows-of-japan.net/.

Jacobs, Jim. *The Burma Railway: One Man's Story* (1947). Privately published.

Kildey, Harold Stephen (Mick) (n.d.). *Reminiscences*. Unpublished manuscript, Private collection of Kildey family.

Lush, John Frederick Douglas (2011–2015). Oral history manuscript/interviews with Carl Johnson. Lush family papers.

Paterson, John. POW Diaries August 1942 – October 1945. Private collection of Janet Paterson AM.

Trumble, Ken. POW War Diary 1942–45. Private collection of Trumble family.

Video Documentaries

Australians War Film Archive (University of NSW), interview with Warrant Officer Desmond Mulcahy, 2/19th Battalion, AIF, 2 May 2003.

Some Came Home: Pacific War Veterans Tell Their Stories of Survival from the Hell Ships, Schindler Entertainment, 2014.

Interviews with the Author

Chapman, Bob. Melbourne, 7 September 2018.

Paterson, Janet. Melbourne, 13 February 2019.

Trumble, Hugh & Michael. Melbourne, 4 March 2020.

INDEX

INDEX

Sakai Prison, Osaka 121
Sakamoto, Mutsujiro 112, 113, 132
Sakura Maru (ship) 21
Sambo *see* Wilsterman, Willem
   Hendrik Louis
Sandakan, Borneo 61–2, 64
Shirriff, Bruce *see* Shirriff, Bunny
Shirriff, Bunny 111, 112–13
sickness, among POWs 90–8
Signals Corps 3–4
   see also 8th Division Signals
Sime Road camp, Singapore 61
Singapore, bombing of 19
   Japanese invasion 33–40
   retreat to 31–2
   surrender to Japanese 40
Singora, Thailand 21
Smith, William 'Nifty' 119–21
sports meeting, at Kobe camp 106–7
Stevens, Ken 71
Stewart, Ian 31–2
Sugamo Jail, Tokyo 180
suicides, of POWs 117
surrender, of Americans to
   Japanese 162
   of Japanese 162
Szilard, Leo, nuclear bomb
   prediction 158

Taiho (ship) 144
Takatori Michi, Kobe, POW camp *see*
   Osaka 5-D Camp, Kobe
Takumi, Kiroshi 21
Takumi Detachment 21–4
Tanagawa camp, Honshu 159, 151–2,
   180, 182
Tanglin Barracks, Singapore 41
Taylor, Harold Burfield 11, 32, 36, 37,
   39, 40
Tengah airfield, Singapore 33
Thai–Burma railway 61, 64
Thomson, Frank 29
Thyer, Jim 7–8, 9, 10, 11, 17, 41
Tibbets, Paul 159
Tojo, Hideki 178, 180

Tokyo Number 4 Branch Camp,
   Naoetsu 65, 73
Tomita, Mr 170–1
Treloar, Colin 'Ike' 21
troopships *see Aquitania*; *Mauretania*;
   Nieuw Amsterdam; *Queen Mary*
Trumble, Florence 5
Trumble, Helen 191
Trumble, Hugh 5
Trumble, Ken 5–6, 12, 52, 185
   assault by guards 112
   and C Force 65, 71
   diary 204
   and firefighting 141–3
   on food drops 165
   homecoming 189, 191, 193
   at Ikuno camp 168, 172
   at Kobe camp 79, 80, 93, 97, 99,
      105, 120, 130
   leaving Ikuno 182
   on liberation uncertainty 162
   at New Osaka Hotel 173–4
   repatriation flight from
      Okinawa 175–6
   transfer to Ikuno 146, 147, 148
Trumble, Robert 5, 189
Tsuji, Masanobu 22, 27, 33
Tyler, Everett 180–1, 182

Unbroken (movie) 74

Vacuum Oil Company 4
Varley, Arthur 36, 40, 41
violence, against POWs 108, 111–18,
   132, 151
Vyner Brooke (ship) 16

Wainwright, Jonathan 46
war crimes, prosecutions for 178–83
Watanabe, Mutsushiro 74
Watson, John 155
Watt, Orm 2
Wavell, Archibald 34–5
Weinberg, Ray 192
Welvaadt, Ben 74

ABOUT THE AUTHOR

Mark Baker is one of Australia's most experienced journalists. He is a former Senior Editor of *The Age*, Editor of *The Canberra Times* and Managing Editor (National) of Fairfax Media. During 13 years as a foreign correspondent for Fairfax, News Corp and *The Financial Times* he had postings in China, Hong Kong, Thailand, Singapore and Papua New Guinea. He covered the wars in Iraq and Afghanistan and was wounded while covering the civil war in Bougainville in the early 1990s. He has also served as Political Editor and Canberra Bureau Chief of *The Age*. Mark Baker is now publisher of the independent online magazine *Inside Story*. His most recent book was *Philip Schuler: The Remarkable Life of One of Australia's Greatest War Correspondents*.